Adolescent Literature as a Complement to the Content Areas

Adolescent Literature as a Complement to the Content Areas

Social Science and the Humanities

Edited by Paula Greathouse,
Joan F. Kaywell, and Brooke Eisenbach

ROWMAN & LITTLEFIELD
Lanham • Boulder • New York • London

Published by Rowman & Littlefield
A wholly owned subsidiary of The Rowman & Littlefield Publishing Group, Inc.
4501 Forbes Boulevard, Suite 200, Lanham, Maryland 20706
www.rowman.com

Unit A, Whitacre Mews, 26–34 Stannary Street, London SE11 4AB

British Library Cataloguing in Publication Information Available

Library of Congress Cataloging-in-Publication Data

Names: Greathouse, Paula, editor. | Kaywell, Joan F., editor. | Eisenbach, Brooke, editor.
Title: Adolescent literature as a complement to the content areas : social science and the humanities / edited by Paula Greathouse, Joan F. Kaywell, and Brooke Eisenbach.
Description: Lanham, Maryland : Rowman & Littlefield, 2017. | Includes bibliographical references and index.
Identifiers: LCCN 2017025258 (print) | LCCN 2017040626 (ebook) | ISBN 9781475838329 (Electronic) | ISBN 9781475838305 (cloth : alk. paper) | ISBN 9781475838312 (pbk. : alk. paper)
Subjects: LCSH: Content area reading. | Language arts—Correlation with content subjects. | Young adult fiction—Study and teaching. | Social sciences—Study and teaching (Secondary) | Humanities—Study and teaching (Secondary) | Interdisciplinary approach in education.
Classification: LCC LB1050.455 (ebook) | LCC LB1050.455 .A36 2017 (print) | DDC 372.47/6—dc23
LC record available at https://lccn.loc.gov/2017025258

Printed in the United States of America

Contents

Preface

Tenth-grader Preston sits at the dining room table—a history textbook and twelve sheets of Cornell Notes sprawled across the glass. He lets out a sigh and mumbles, "Here goes nothing" under his breath. For an hour he sits there, trying to make sense of the information in an attempt to answer a series of questions posed at the end of the chapter. The rustling of papers grows louder, and a thump echoes throughout the house as his fists hit the table. I (Paula) immediately check on him and find his head down, buried in crossed arms. "What's wrong?" I ask my son. For almost fifteen minutes he vents about how difficult the textbook is to read, how all they do is take notes directly from the book or from the teacher's lecture, and how he once loved history but it is no longer interesting to him. When he finishes talking, he shoves the papers and textbook into his backpack and heads to bed—assignment incomplete!

Preston's experience is similar to that of many adolescent learners. On a daily basis, students are required to independently navigate textbooks to learn content. Today, the textbooks utilized to accomplish this feat are not simplistic in any fashion. They are collections of in-depth, sophisticated text with challenging assessments attached. Reading researchers Daniels and Zemelman (2003) posit,

> School textbooks exemplify "inconsiderate" or "unfriendly" text. They are storage systems for information, giant compendiums of data. They are intentionally "content-overloaded" with facts, dates, formulas, and taxonomies. They introduce vocabulary and concepts at a blinding rate. Highly structured and orderly, they pack information into carefully labeled slots as closely as possible.
>
> (p. 36)

Reading research also denotes that textbooks fail in motivating students to read or learn (Beck & McKeown, 1991). Yet many of today's content area teachers continue to use textbooks as the primary source of content information.

Adolescent Literature as a Complement to the Content Areas was created based on three assumptions: (1) textbooks are the primary source of information being utilized in content area classrooms; (2) content area teachers are familiar with both their content and literacy standards; and (3) most content area teachers are not familiar with adolescent or young adult (YA) literature and those who are, are unsure how to include it in their content area as a tool for developing content knowledge and literacy. This book provides content area teachers the frameworks for teaching YA literature as a means to deepen students' understanding of content while practicing literacy in tandem.

Why should content area teachers include YA literature alongside textbooks? First, textbooks used in most content area classrooms are so far removed from students' lives that relevance and meaningfulness are often not spotlighted. When students see no relevance of the content to their lives, engagement waiver and intrinsic motivation to learn is hampered. Adolescent or YA literature, however, features characters, plots, and themes that are relevant to the lives of secondary students. Pairing YA titles with textbook reading can promote greater connection and reader engagement. Second, most textbooks used within secondary content areas are written at a level that makes them difficult for students to tackle. As a result, students struggle with comprehension and often turn to skimming instead of critical reading. The reading levels of most YA literature books are within a range of ease that students should have little struggle with comprehension. When concepts are placed in familiar contexts, students draw on their prior knowledge to create meaning, thereby making learning more accessible and sustainable. As such, YA literature provides students a familiar medium through which to learn content, practice literacy, and enhance their world. Finally, course textbooks provide only one perspective. Students need opportunities to explore content concepts through multiple perspectives. Young adult literature features a diverse array of characters, settings, and perspectives.

In our standards-driven classrooms, making concepts relevant and meaningful to students while meeting the requirements of our curriculum can be a challenging task. The need to now develop student's literacy skills and practices in tandem with learning content has many content area teachers concerned (Moore, Bean, Birdyshaw, & Rycik, 1999). Although a valuable tool, Edington (1988) argues, "A textbook cannot lend itself to the same sort of detail, passion, or interest that a story can generate" (p. 121). Readence, Bean, and Baldwin (2004) support this, maintaining novels have the potential to illuminate concepts across all disciplines in a way that textbooks cannot.

When content is presented in adolescent worlds, it becomes more relevant and meaningful, which generates stronger content appeal for secondary students (Schallert & Roser, 2004). When adolescent or YA books are read as a complement to content area textbooks, students become engaged learners. Students learn to synthesize concepts across a range of texts (Bean, 2003), while providing focus and coherence to content area instruction (Austin, Thompson, & Beckman, 2005). Beyond content, YA literature also offers opportunities for students to explore and dialogue about "a wide range of societal issues that cut across content areas, including conflict, violence, ethical decisions, ecological issues, and family life" (Bean, 2003, p. 3). In other words, YA literature holds the potential to connect content to the human experience.

There are two givens when it comes to reading in the content areas. First, we know that when students have a difficult time reading and comprehending a course textbook, they become disengaged with the content and unmotivated to learn. We also know that we do not teach in homogenous classes, yet students often all work from the same text. Given the variety of YA literature available today, reading this genre to complement the content also offers teacher opportunities to differentiate instruction (Schallert & Roser, 2004). According to Fang (2014), "Compared to traditional textbooks, trade books [adolescent literature] are better able to accommodate the needs of students with diverse backgrounds, interests, needs, and reading levels" (p. 274).

Reading YA literature in content area classrooms provides access points for students to practice reading like content area experts—scientists, mathematicians, historians, psychologists, and artists, and so on—an approach often limited in content area classrooms. Positioning students as readers in this way helps develop critical literacy, as concepts are explored at deeper levels. Literacies differ across content areas. For example, reading in math is not the same as reading in history. Each requires different approaches, ones that entail a shift in the way students read. Giving students opportunities to read like scientists, mathematicians, historians, psychologists, and artists, as they explore content has the potential to move their thinking and understandings in monumental ways. In science, the reading of YA literature extends experimental involvement as students come to examine scientific concepts as potential life-impacting factors (Bragaw, Gragow, & Smith, 1995). In math, students can be encouraged to draw on imagination as they solve problems presented in the text as a way to consider the possibilities of math in their world and future (Koellner, Wallace, & Swackhamer, 2009). In social studies, the integration of literature, both fictional and factual, is said to help transport students to other cultures, places, and eras, offering them multiple perspectives of the same event (Krey, 1998).

The need to develop students' literacy skills and practices in tandem with learning content has been a growing concern for many content area teachers. Teachers of all content areas are now required to address students' literacy development within their discipline—what was once believed to be the responsibility of the English teacher has become the responsibility of *all* teachers. When faced with this expectation, content area teachers often ask, *How can we do both?* While it is apparent that literature holds the key to unlocking the common rift between content and literacy-driven instruction, how can today's content area teachers seamlessly infuse narrative texts into an already overwhelming curriculum?

Research in the study of adolescent literature, or young adult (YA) literature, supports the use of YA literature within content area classrooms as a means of developing content knowledge and literacy. In conversations with content area teachers, few appear to be utilizing this valuable resource. This absence has been attributed to not only the educator's lack of knowledge and exposure to YA literature but also understanding effective instructional approaches for including these texts within their already abundant curriculum. In other words, content area educators are still not clear on ways in which they can incorporate YA literature and engage students in activities and dialogues about content while supporting literacy practices. This book is intended to fill this gap by providing frameworks for content area teachers in the inclusion of literature, specifically YA literature, as a means to develop content knowledge and literacy practices.

We envision teachers, both in-service and preservice, as well as teacher educators utilizing this text as a means of professional development and thoughtful inclusion of YA literature to address literacy development in the content area classroom. The book's content lends itself to the exploration of concepts in relevant, meaningful ways that will engage and motivate adolescent learners.

REFERENCES

Austin, R. A., Thompson, D. R., & Beckmann, C. E. (2005). Exploring measurement concepts through literature: Natural links across disciplines. *Mathematics Teaching in the Middle School, 10*, 218–224.

Bean, T. W. (2003). *Using young-adult literature to enhance comprehension in the content areas*. Naperville, IL: North Central Regional Educational Laboratory.

Beck, I. L., & McKeown, M. G. (1991). Social studies texts are hard to understand: Mediating some of the difficulties. *Language Arts, 68*(6), 482–490.

Bragow, D., Gragow, K. A., & Smith, E. (1995). Back to the future: Toward curriculum integration. *Middle School Journal, 27*(2), 39–46.

Daniels, H. and Zemelman, S. (2003). Out with textbooks, in with learning. *Educational Leadership 61*(4), 36–40.

Edington, W. D. (1998). The use of children's literature in middle school social studies: What research does and does not show. *The Clearing House, 72*(2), 121–126.

Fang, Z. (2014). Disciplinary literacy in science: Developing science literacy through trade books. *Journal of Adolescent & Adult Literacy, 57*(4), 274–278.

Koellner, K., Wallace, F. H., & Swackhamer, L. (2009). Integrating literature to support the development of mathematics in middle school. *Middle School Journal, 41*(2), 30–39.

Krey, D. M. (1998). *Children's literature in social studies: Teaching to the standards.* NCSS Bulletin 95. Washington, DC: National Council for the Social Studies.

Moore, D. W., Bean, T. W., Birdyshaw, D., & Rycik, J. A. (1999). *Adolescent literacy: A position statement.* Newark, DE: International Reading Association.

Readence, J. E., Bean, T. W., & Baldwin, R. S. (2004). *Content area literacy: An integrated approach* (8th ed.). Dubuque, IA: Kendall/Hunt.

Schallert, D. L., & Roser, N. L. (2004). The role of textbooks and trade books in content area instruction. In D. Lapp, J. Flood, & N. Farnan (Eds.), *Content area reading and learning*, 27–38. London, UK: Routledge.

Acknowledgments

Paula Greathouse: I would first like to thank Joan Kaywell for her support and mentorship. It all began eight years ago when I walked into your office seeking guidance. I will always be grateful for your encouragement and friendship.

Next I would like to thank Brooke Eisenbach for your friendship and willingness to be my partner. I never could have made this journey without you.

A very special thanks to my husband for understanding why I couldn't talk to you all those nights, even though we were in the same room!

Joan F. Kaywell: I must thank all of the English language arts (ELA) teachers who have used *Adolescent Literature as a Complement to the Classics*, Volumes 1 through 5 since its first publication in 1993. Because of you, young people are reading more today than ever before.

I would also like to thank the authors who write young adult (YA) fiction and nonfiction. Without you, ELA teachers would still be teaching only the classics of literature and would not have the breadth and depth that your writing offers.

Finally, I would also like to thank Paula Greathouse and Brooke Eisenbach, two former doctoral students, who have picked up where I have left off. You two give me hope for the future because we need a nation of readers more now than ever before.

Brooke Eisenbach: I, too, would like to thank Joan Kaywell for her guidance and mentorship over the years. From the moment I walked into her undergraduate young adult literature course to having her support me through my doctoral program and dissertation, she has continued to serve as an inspirational touchstone. Thank you for your support through the years.

I would like to thank Paula Greathouse for your continued friendship. We make a terrific team, and I wouldn't have it any other way!

Finally, I would like to thank my husband and daughter for your constant love and encouragement. Thank you for believing in me and loving me unconditionally through the most stressful of circumstances. I wouldn't be where I am today if it weren't for you.

Introduction

In order to ensure both content and literacy standards are being addressed within each of the instructional approaches presented throughout this text, chapters are written in teams consisting of one literacy expert and one content area expert. In addition, the instructional approaches presented within each chapter draw on research-based practices and are aligned with both content and literacy standards that will lead students to the acquisition of deeper knowledge of the content and enhanced literacy practices.

Contributors have scaffolded their approaches to include pre-, during-, and after-reading activities that address both content and literacy standards and provide readers with suggested extension activities designed to move students toward a deeper critical literacy. In addition, each chapter offers annotated lists of additional YA novels that spotlight-specific content topics for teacher and student consideration.

The first chapter is written by a librarian to explain how librarians are an important resource for content area teachers. Media specialists can assist content area teachers in selecting adolescent literature or young adult (YA) books and provide assistance in how they may be used to enhance instruction. After that introductory chapter, this book is organized into two sections: Connecting Social Sciences and Literacy followed by Connecting the Humanities—Art, Drama, and Music—and Literacy. The chapters connecting the social sciences with literacy are organized chronologically according to the event: the Revolutionary War, the Depression and the Dust Bowl, World War II, Civil Right Movement, and contemporary social issues. The chapters connecting the humanities with literacy are in the order mentioned previously. The last chapter shows how YA literature can positively affect adolescents in a psychology class.

While each section in this book focuses on a specific content area, teachers can easily adapt the strategies and approaches presented within each chapter to fit their particular classroom context. There are numerous opportunities for cross-disciplinary study, and each instructional approach presented is student-centered and supported by research.

Chapter 1

Collaborating with School Librarians to Guide Content Area Literacies Using Young Adult Literature

Julie Stepp

In a book filled with content area and literacy experts exploring young adult (YA) literature's use in various content areas, a reminder: your school's librarian is there to help. Gone are the days of a school librarian hoarding resources and telling people to shush. Instead, contemporary school librarians lead from the middle. They find ways to collaborate with teachers in discovering resources and other teaching needs, helping students to find the best books and resources for assignments, assisting teachers and students with creating and sharing projects, and supporting principals with the impact of cross-curricular expectations. The librarian is an expert and wonderful resource for collaborating on using YA literature in the classroom.

THE DISCOVERY AND INVESTIGATION OF YOUNG ADULT LITERATURE

Historically, libraries have existed as places to organize resources and information for people to find and use. Within and outside the walls of the modern-day library, students, teachers, and others expand their searches for information beyond books and library catalogs. Libraries continue to be important sources of materials, including YA literature, and require librarians to build strong and useful collections based on well-defined collection of development policies. Discovering exceptional titles worth having in a school library collection takes time and requires a discrepant, keen reviewer. Many school librarians, rather than finding themselves as the sole deciders, rely on collection development input that may include several other resources:

• Suggestions from teachers, students, other librarians, administrators, and even parents

- Content area standards, especially as more book publishers and distributors incorporate information on which titles will fit certain standards or subject areas
- Book reviews in respected and established journals such as *School Library Journal, ALAN, Booklist*, and *Choice*—all of which go through an editorial process
- Online user reviews, within reason, found on Amazon and universal bookshelf catalogs such as Goodreads and LibraryThing.

A well-balanced collection will include contemporary YA literature that is diverse in both content (genres, forms of prose, text complexity) and format (print, e-books, audiobooks).

With a collection firmly established (yet ever growing), the investigation of a plethora of possibilities when using YA literature begins with finding the *right* book(s): What possibilities are there? What books would work best in what situation and/or content area? Are there books that would be useful across multiple content areas? It would be nice if every school librarian had the time to read every book that became part of a collection, but that just can't happen; instead, an effective librarian learns more about YA books through journal and online summaries and reviews. Within the school setting, a librarian conducts formal and informal discussions with readers of the library's books, learning more about the content of the stories and their characters. These same techniques may also be used by teachers in determining the best books to use in their classrooms. In addition, librarians encourage students to investigate and to read independently, to self-select books that interest them. When truly becoming independent readers, students engage in discussion about reading and what they are reading with educators and each other (Kent & Simpson, 2012). This in turn creates a community of readers. In nurturing these reading communities, teachers may find the next great book(s) to use in their classroom through collaboration with their school media specialist.

Information Literacy

When using YA literature in various content areas, exploration begins with the *right* book for the overall unit: in social science, the Civil Rights Movement through the eyes of Emmett Till in *Mississippi Trial 1955* (2003) by Chris Crowe and through the eyes of Claudette Colvin in *Twice toward Justice* (2009) by Phillip Hoose, or the social justice issue of immigration in *Crossing the Wire* (2007) by Will Hobbs that puts a human face on the political issue; in the arts, exploring music in *The Last True Love Story* (2016) by Brendan Kiely, personal expression through art in *The Eyes of van Gogh*

(2007) by Cathryn Clinton, or character strengths in *Whale Talk* (2001) by Chris Cructher.

Authors do not write YA literature for readers to answer comprehension questions or learn facts (Wolk, 2009); rather, they write to tell a good story. It is up to the classroom community to explore beyond the story, and the library affords both the resources and assistance with these resources.

School libraries have undergone extreme changes in the past twenty years. Much of this change has come through the addition of Internet-based resources such as library catalogs and periodical databases; newspapers, news outlets, bloggers, and aggregators; previously printed reference sources including atlases, dictionaries, and encyclopedias; and the overabundance of freely given information and misinformation. School librarians have had to become experts in finding, using, and evaluating information in an exponentially larger set of resources than ever before. Even more exciting is that the focus in literacy and inquiry has made the strongest case ever for librarians as learning (inquiry) leaders and for the indispensability of vibrant and deeply instructionally relevant library programs in *all* schools (Harada & Coatney, 2014).

Collaboration

Bear in mind that librarians, just as content area teachers, have their own standards; currently we use the *Standards for the 21st Century Learner* (American Association of School Librarians [AASL], 2007). These standards, usually associated with information literacy, comprise strategies used in the inquiry process at any grade level. Librarians may also have a working knowledge of other content standards but will rely on the expertise of teachers in their various disciplines for student expectations. The library standards ask librarians to lead learners in using skills, resources, and tools to

- inquire, think critically, and gain knowledge;
- draw conclusions, make informed decisions and apply knowledge to new situations, and create new knowledge;
- share knowledge and participate ethically and productively as members of our democratic society; and
- pursue personal and aesthetic growth. (AASL, 2007)

The progression through these standards helps students become independent learners and should be practiced multiple times throughout their time in school.

Within the AASL standards, collaboration between the librarian and teachers only magnifies expectations of independent learners. There are five entry points to collaboration—*building community, intellectual freedom, multiple literacies, curriculum,* and *technology*—that will assist content area teachers in connecting with the various lessons found in the following chapters in this book.

Building Community

In librarianship, the classification of libraries depends on what the community of users includes. In school libraries, this of course includes students and teachers, but also administrators, school staff, and even parents and families. The school community subdivides into smaller communities based on learning needs, class level, sports and clubs, and numerous other schemas. The library provides not only places for these subcommunities to engage with each other but also a place to create and support community.

Building a *community of readers* proves to be the foundation in much of the research on using YA literature in school settings. Students who deeply engage as readers do so through choice (self-selection); diverse and contemporary collections; and discussion with other students, teachers, and librarians about the books they have read (Ivey, 2014; Roberts, 2006). Engaged readers understand more socially, are better able to discuss what they have read, and are engaged beyond the expectations of classroom work (Ivey & Johnston, 2013). They also recognize that reading will be different depending on the text, the reader, and circumstances for reading. Furthermore, they support each other through ideas such as Pennac's (1996) Reader's Bill of Rights:

1. The right not to read
2. The right to skip pages
3. The right to not finish
4. The right to reread
5. The right to read anything
6. The right to escapism
7. The right to read anywhere
8. The right to browse
9. The right to read out loud
10. The right to not defend your tastes

At the heart of reading communities, everyone values reading. Libraries continue to exist and thrive because of all sorts of reading communities such as classes, book clubs (made of students and teachers alike), and book reviewers and even informal sharing of texts. Teachers who take advantage of these reading communities engage and build beyond their classroom expectations and acknowledge lifelong readers are lifelong learners.

Building on that, the library absolutely promotes a *community of learners*. Through the different subject areas within a school, expectations for student learning create learners who want to delve deeper into the content. For example, a group of readers who delve into historical fiction, in two separate classes—one reading *Mississippi Trial, 1955* (Crowe, 2003) and the other *Claudette Colvin: Twice towards Justice* (Hoose, 2009)—may create something entirely unique. These stories speak to very different events in the early years of the Civil Rights Movement. The library serves as a place where students from each class could come together and merge their understandings from each story and learn even more. The collection and access to appropriate online resources assists with learning community members' multiple reading levels and objectives.

Lastly, a relatively new concept for libraries is a *community of makers*. Makerspaces quite literally means "spaces to make things" and inspire students' hands-on investigation and collaborative learning. Librarians provide students access to space, materials, tools, and technologies to facilitate this community of makers. Here, students from different grade levels who have an interest in the humanities may upcycle materials to create/produce and then display/perform art inspired by *Eyes of Van Gogh* (Clinton, 2007), *Drama High* (Sokolove, 2013), or *The Last True Love Story* (Kiely, 2016). Others impassioned by their study of *Claudette Colvin: Twice toward Justice* (Hoose, 2009) or *Emmet Till* (Crowe, 2003) may want to create an antibullying campaign for their schools. The possibilities are endless, and librarians are here to help.

Intellectual Freedom

Intellectual freedom is the right of every individual to both seek and receive information from all points of view without restriction (AASL, 2010). When libraries support this right, students experience free access to all expressions of ideas through which any and all sides of a question, cause, or movement may be explored. School librarians guide students in accessing information in different forms, finding and obtaining relevant information, and evaluating the information and the process (AASL, 2007). This includes the librarian's dependence on teachers and students with the selection of resources as discussed earlier.

Libraries, more than any other entity, prevail as the place where intellectual freedom is supported and taught. In fact, the American Library Association (ALA) actively advocates for intellectual freedom as "a core value of the library profession, and a basic right in our democratic society" (ALA, n.d.). While the AASL, a major division of ALA, does recognize the boundaries of participating in a school setting, school librarians are encouraged to recognize the difference between being "professional selectors" or "self-imposed censors" (AASL, 2010) and to be responsible in introducing our emerging citizens to the world of information. Some titles shared in this book tie directly to essential ideas of intellectual freedom and how people have been denied access to information such as in *Mississippi Trial* and *Claudette Colvin* in regard to Jim Crow laws.

In addition, just as the ALA and AASL encourage librarians to work with resources and information ethically, librarians encourage students to use information ethically. Librarians recognize that "ethical behavior in the use of information must be taught . . . students must be taught to seek diverse perspectives, gather and use information ethically, and use social tools responsibly and safely" (AASL, 2007). Imagine the discussions of ethics as it pertains to how we learn about mental illness in *Whale Talk* (Crutcher, 2001) or *Eyes of Van Gogh* (Clinton, 2007).

It would be thoughtless not to recognize that intellectual freedom also covers books that have been challenged and banned, a couple of which appear in this book: *Whale Talk* and *All American Boys* (Reynolds & Kiely, 2015). The ALA and other organizations defend the rights of all readers to have access to books and other texts despite the content. In fact, the ALA organizes Banned Book Week each year, a campaign that promotes awareness of challenges and celebrates that we live in a society that strives to allow readers their books without censure.

Multiple Literacies

The National Council of Teachers of English (NCTE) defines *literacy* as "collections of cultural and communicative practices shared among members of particular groups" (NCTE, 2013). Multiple literacies explore the ability to understand, analyze, utilize, and evaluate not only textual but also visual, digital, informational, and technological literacies. An effective librarian helps students read, read more, read better, and read for a lifetime (Achterman, 2010). The librarian assists teachers and students with multiple literacies by

- modeling and promoting a love of reading;
- collecting and providing access to diverse and multimodal resources;
- deepening teachers' and administrators' understanding of changes in multiple literacies; and
- collaborating with teachers to plan, teach, and evaluate lessons that promote multiple literacies.

Within the titles discussed in this book, one of the best areas for librarians to assist learning is with prior knowledge or pre-reading. This may come through students using multiple literacies such as visual literacies of Van Gogh's paintings before reading *Eyes of Van Gogh*, aural literacies with songs and lyrics alongside *The Last True Love Story*, and digital literacy in online pictures of Emmett Till and Claudette Colvin for their respective stories. The library provides a judgment-free zone for student inquiry into necessary background knowledge for the books they read.

Graphic novels deserve a bit more attention here as well. Gareth Hinds, who describes himself as a sequential artist, adapts classics such as *The Odyssey* and *Macbeth* into graphic novels. In a talk at an Assembly for Literature of Adolescents of NCTE (ALAN) workshop, Hinds stated that one of the major reasons graphic novels support the literacy needs of our students is that readers must slow down to read both the text and the graphics/images of the story. A librarian can be asked to aid readers who struggle with creating images in their minds as they read text, or assist readers who decode words but need help with making meaning of the graphics/images. A school librarian guides reluctant readers to the graphic novels section and supports teachers' subjects by purchasing and sharing the best of this growing format.

Curriculum

Curriculum has been defined in various ways but basically describes much of what occurs in the classroom setting. While librarians may not be experts in a specific curriculum or content area, their expertise in inquiry and instruction (a majority of states require they be licensed teachers) supplies the basis for collaboration in inquiry-based learning. The school librarian who takes a leadership role in the school's global view in the learning community helps build and sustain a culture of collaboration with

- teachers by co-teaching based on the teachers' goals for learning and by guiding student inquiry,
- students in regard to finding and evaluating resources and in learning types of inquiry,
- administrators' school climate and inquiry goals, and
- caregivers who need homework help and have questions about inquiry (Harada & Coatney, 2014; Kimmel, 2012).

With administrative and school community support, librarians may be the key to cross-curricular learning, especially with strategies such as those found with makerspaces. For example, a makerspace may include art supplies for students wanting to express themselves as in *Eyes of Van Gogh*. The key components for makerspaces are that they have a variety of materials and allow students to direct their own projects and learning.

One area of support that acts as the basis of any library is the influence a librarian can have on literacy in the school. Librarians are the cheerleaders of reading, encouraging students to find texts that intrigue and excite them. Libraries exist as places for every genre and format of books and access to materials online and in-house. They support the elements of literacy in every content area in regard to vocabulary, multiple literacies, and critical thinking.

Finally, librarians provide curriculum support through the tools they teach and share with students. For example, while exploring aspects of Claudette Colvin, students may want to try a variety of graphic organizers. The library provides not only the space to explore but also some expertise in possible organizers to use for different expectations. Most importantly, libraries exist as a place to further learning and reading: leaping from *Whale Talk* to find more authors who tell hard-hitting stories with sports slant such as Walter Dean Myers and Matthew Quick or finding Marilyn Nelson's novel in verse *A Wreath for Emmett Till* (2005) to accompany *Mississippi Trial* and extending that to include Shannon Hitchcock's *Ruby Lee and Me* (2016) that covers school integration with the mention of Freedom Riders, Emmett Till, and Brown vs. Board of Education. The possibilities of engaging beyond one book or one assignment become endless.

Technology

Technology has become part of nearly every aspect of the lives of librarians, even changing the expectations of what a school library offers. Librarians, as teachers, have varying levels of expertise in how technologies work but make the effort to use technologies for inquiry, teaching, and collaboration. Teachers may learn about online resources, adaptive technologies, or devices from the librarian; they may also be learning alongside them. Teachers should take both opportunities to collaborate and explore, seeing how student learning might be enhanced rather than using technology for the sake of having it.

Technology in a library may include access to the Internet, use of laptops and/or tablets, makerspace technologies such as 3D printers, even sewing machines. Here are some examples of how technology could benefit some of the titles found in this book. In *All American Boys*, readers consider two perspectives of an event. Every day, we are bombarded with multiple perspectives but also purposeful misinformation and fake news. Libraries subsist as places to locate and use information, and librarians assist students with their examination of information. No place is this more necessary than on the Internet—a place filled with blogs, news outlets, and other mass media. Now is an opportune time to investigate perspectives as seen in *All American Boys*, with its white police brutality on a black youth, by recommending Kekla Magoon's *How It Went Down* (2015). As mentioned in the chapter using the *Eyes of Van Gogh*, Google's Art Project (www.google.com/culturalinstitute/about/artproject/) opens access to a massive amount of art and information about the art and artists. The library may be a place for access to this project but could also be where classes view pieces on a large screen or print out a particular piece to use in a presentation.

Lastly, at least for the examples here, there are some online tools that assist students with in-depth exploration of stories. Storyboardthat.com allows students to create and share digital storytelling, study literary elements, and visualize story components to learn more about the content; a similar site is toondoo.com. Mural.co supports online, collaborative brainstorming, similar to graffiti mapping. Online brainstorming may also be organized through semantic mapping as on bubbl.us. While teachers use these sites within the classroom and/or in the library, the librarian may be a co-teacher and give insight to using these resources and others.

P.S. FOR LIBRARIANS

My hope for fellow librarians is that you will read this chapter and think, "Hey, I have some of this happening in our school and library!" If so, let this section be a pat on the back for a job well done; however, if you are a librarian feeling frustrated and unnerved by the crazy amount of change in the expectations, let me reassure you that change will happen and you can gain in the amazingness of the library in your charge. Here is a "to-do" list to guide you.

Flexible Spaces

Contemporary school libraries owe it to the school community to be vibrant and noisy and maybe a little chaotic. Imagine a library with shelves, tables, and chairs on lockable wheels that allow a librarian to reimagine how her or his community uses the space based on the needs that month, week, or even day. Even with smaller spaces, librarians find ways of flexing library space by having makerspace resources in bins or carts, displaying projects on top of shelving, and taking time to be outside of the library to work with teachers and others. Some libraries are changing space and expectations by adding (or becoming) a learning commons (Murray, 2015). No matter how the library looks, it should be a place where students can read, converse, inquire, research, plan, and solve problems.

Julie Stepp

Appreciate Some Library Science Theory

S. R. Ranganathan invented the term *library science* and formulated five demonstrable "laws" founded in observation and analysis (Gorman, 1998). These *Five Laws of Library Science* speak to the experience of every user:

1. Books are for use.
2. Every reader his or her book.
3. Every book its reader.
4. Save the time of the reader.
5. The library is a growing organism.

Michael Gorman recognized the enthusiasm and insight of Ranganathan's "laws" but wanted to think of them in a more current setting. He generated five new "laws" as a way of evaluating our current expectations:

1. Libraries serve humanity.
2. Respect all forms by which knowledge is communicated.
3. Use technology intelligently to enhance service.
4. Protect free access to knowledge.
5. Honor the past and create the future.

Both librarians' writings provide a framework for how we, as librarians, should think about serving our communities. It will do us all well to think deeply on the "laws" and internalize their expectations of a librarian and the school's library.

Network

Some school districts nurture networking possibilities—school librarians from every school have the chance to meet a couple of times a semester, and a coordinator at the central office oversees the expectations of the libraries within the district—other districts, not so much. It may be up to an individual to engage in finding or creating a librarian network. Find out how librarians in the district might best engage in on-site meetings and online meetings, through blogs or other conversational sites, or simply using e-mail. Districts that have successful networks will share ideas that have worked for them. Realize, too, numerous public librarians are eager to work with school librarians and the school community. Finally, active participation in local, state, and national library organizations where people, ideas, and action unite indispensably connects librarians.

Collaboration (With a Dash of Advocacy)

In my teaching with preservice librarians, some of whom will take the place of an imperious or old-school librarian, I encourage my students to work small when starting collaboration in their school. The process might start with an English teacher and a history teacher, a couple of teachers with whom they are friends, or some other small group of teachers. Together, they explore what the librarian can do for them and their students and vice versa. Pretty soon, other teachers will be curious (or jealous) and will want to be a part of the collaboration. Making a school community change happen through the library will not be an overnight success; rather, it will succeed with a strong advocacy plan. The ALA encourages advocacy for school libraries, including creating plans for advocacy through *Toolkit for Promoting School Library Programs*. It is also important to note that teachers know they need help. There are just not enough hours in a day to keep up with the demands of teaching. As a librarian, recognize that teachers may not know to ask you for assistance and may not know the right questions to ask. Think of ways you can let teachers know how you can enhance their teaching and strengthen student learning. Play to your strengths. Take time outside of the library and meet them on their own turf.

CONCLUSION

Just as YA literature continues to grow as a viable resource for teachers, librarians continue to flourish as collaborators, resource finders, and sounding boards for teachers. Using the ideas and initiatives discussed in this chapter will strengthen possibilities that will enhance teaching endeavors as well as student engagement through the core of the school.

REFERENCES

Achterman, D. (2010). Literacy leadership and the school library. In S. Coatney (Ed.), *The many faces of school library leadership*, 67–84. Westport, CT: Libraries Unlimited.

American Association of School Librarians (2007). *Standards for the 21st century learner*. Retrieved from http://www.ala.org/aasl/standards-guidelines/learning-standards.

American Association of School Librarians (2010). *What is intellectual freedom?* Retrieved from http://www.ala.org/aasl/advocacy/if.

American Library Association (n.d.). *Intellectual freedom*. Retrieved from http://www.ala.org/advocacy/intfreedom.

American Library Association (n.d.). *Toolkit for promoting school library programs.* Retrieved from http://www.ala.org/aasl/advocacy/tools/toolkits/promoting/plan.

Clinton, C. (2007). *The eyes of van Gogh.* Somerville, MA: Candlewick.

Crowe, C. (2003). *Mississippi trial, 1955.* New York: Speak.

Crutcher, C. (2001). *Whale talk.* New York: Greenwillow Books.

Gorman, M. (1998). *Our singular strengths: Meditations for librarians,* 61. Chicago, IL: American Library Association.

Harada, V. H., & Coatney, S. (Eds.) (2014). *Inquiry and the common core: Librarians and teachers designing teaching for learning.* Westport, CT: Libraries Unlimited.

Hitchcock, S. (2016). *Ruby Lee and me.* New York: Scholastic.

Hoose, P. M. (2009). *Claudette Colvin: Twice toward justice.* New York: Melanie Kroupa Books/Farrar Straus Giroux.

Ivey, G. (2014). The social side of engaged reading for young adolescents. *Reading Teacher, 68*(3), 165–171.

Ivey, G., & Johnston, P. H. (2013). Engagement with young adult literature: Outcomes and processes. *Reading Research Quarterly, 48*(3), 255–275.

Kent, A. M., & Simpson, J. L. (2012). The power of literature: Establishing and enhancing the young adolescent classroom community. *Reading Improvement, 49*(1), 28–32.

Kiely, B. (2016). *The last true love story.* New York: Margaret K. McElderry Books.

Kimmel, S. C. (2012). Collaboration as school reform: Are there patterns in the chaos of planning with teachers? *School Library Research, 15,* 1–16.

Magoon, K. (2015). *How it went down.* New York: Henry Holt and Company, LLC.

Murray, E. (2015). Piloting the learning commons: Co-teaching and collaboration between a classroom teacher and a teacher librarian. *Teacher Librarian, 43*(1), 18–24.

National Council of Teachers of English (2013). *The NCTE definition of 21st century literacies.* Retrieved from http://www.ncte.org/positions/statements/21stcentdefinition.

Nelson, M. (2005). *A wreath for Emmett Till.* Boston, MA: Houghton Mifflin.

Pennac, D. (1996). *Better than life.* Toronto, Canada: Coach House Press.

Reynolds, J., & Kiely, B. (2015). *All American boys.* New York: Atheneum.

Roberts, J. (2006). Building a community of high school readers. *Knowledge Quest, 35*(1), 24–29.

Sokolove, M. (2013). *Drama high: The incredible true story of a brilliant teacher, a struggling town, and the magic of theater.* New York: Riverhead Books.

Wolk, S. (2009). Reading for a better world: Teaching for social responsibility with young adult literature. *Journal of Adolescent & Adult Literacy, 52*(8), 664–673.

Chapter 2

The Habits of a Nation: Reading *Chains* in Middle School Social Studies

Gretchen Rumohr-Voskuil and Luke Rumohr

Teachers hold a collective responsibility to encourage students toward pleasure reading. The value of pleasure reading is rarely discussed in the social studies classroom, but should be acknowledged here, given that it can positively influence students' "educational attainment" and "social mobility" (Sullivan & Brown, 2013, p. 37). Unfortunately, pleasure reading can conflict with the goal to have students connect to United States history using pictures, primary sources, and media, which are not necessarily written to accommodate the interests and reading levels of middle schoolers. Social studies students are asked to analyze historical texts, make inferences, and consider historical significance, but if they are not connecting as readers to these sources, it is unlikely that they will understand fully or be motivated to explore or engage further. Thus, there is value in high-interest, historically accurate fiction for the middle school social studies classroom. Fortunately, Laurie Halse Anderson's *Chains* (2008), described as "historically accurate within an inch of its life," certainly fits such a description (Bird, 2008). Anderson begins each of her forty-five chapters with epigraphs that utilize primary sources from the Revolutionary War period, welding a riveting plot with historically relevant text. *Chains* received the Scott O'Dell Award for Historical Fiction, was in the top ten of Black History Books for Youth in 2009, and gained a National Book Award nomination, earning recognition for its literary merit as well as its appeal to young readers. All of these factors point to *Chains* as a rich curricular resource that can further students' textual enjoyment, discussion, and exploration in U.S. history classrooms.

CHAINS BY LAURIE HALSE ANDERSON (313 PP.)

Chains is the first novel in the *Seeds of America* trilogy that focuses on the issue of slavery in the context of the Revolutionary War. Since students

13

may be more accustomed to discussing slavery in the context of the Civil War, *Chains* can provide a broader understanding of the issue of slavery. This novel features Isabel, a thirteen-year-old African American slave who, along with her sister Ruth, is owned by the Locktons, a cruel Loyalist couple. Although fellow slave Curzon suggests that Isabel can gain her freedom by spying for the Patriots, Isabel is fearfully loyal to her owners. Such loyalty turns to anger when the Locktons sell Ruth to another family. With this anger and determination to fight for her own freedom as well as Ruth's, Isabel joins the Patriot cause.

BEFORE READING *CHAINS*

Connecting middle school students to the institution of slavery is essential in understanding the foundations of U.S. history. Prior to reading *Chains*, show students a photo of Monticello, Thomas Jefferson's famed residence. Without giving away the location, the teacher can ask students what and where this place is and to whom it belonged. After revealing the location (Virginia) and owner (Thomas Jefferson), the teacher can share Jefferson's Declaration of Independence, highlighting specifically, "We hold these truths to be self-evident, that all men are created equal, that they are endowed by their Creator with certain unalienable Rights, that among these are Life, Liberty and the pursuit of Happiness." Kylene Beers and Bob Probst's (2015) close reading techniques can be utilized here, as with any primary documents throughout the reading of *Chains*, as the teacher rereads and asks students to identify any contrasts or contradictions they observe, or absolute and extreme language, in the effort to comprehend and engage with this text more fully. After considering the Declaration of Independence, students can view *Unchained Memories*, an HBO documentary produced in 2003.

Available on YouTube, *Unchained Memories* remasters accounts of former slaves found in the Works Projects Administration (WPA) Slave Narrative Collection. Narrated by Whoopi Goldberg and performed by well-known actors such as Oprah Winfrey and Angela Bassett, these accounts serve as poignant reminders of the atrocities committed in the United States' early days. Utilizing a simple format with strong historical imagery, a teacher can very quickly and efficiently move students from Jefferson's words into the harsh realities of the world of slavery. We strongly recommend that teachers preview the material with your middle schoolers in mind as some graphic, yet crucial, content is presented. With this caution in mind, suggested excerpts include 23:00–26:00, which explicitly describes the beating of a slave as well as 50:00–53:00, which details the horrors of a slave auction.

Having students read and briefly discuss Paul Finkelman's short *New York Times* essay "The Monster of Monticello" (2012), students are introduced to the fact that Thomas Jefferson owned slaves. By connecting Jefferson's Monticello to these film excerpts, the teacher can raise questions regarding what conflicts exist between a document like the Declaration of Independence and Jefferson's participation in slavery's horrors. Going further, the class can find and explore, archived newspaper ads detailing the capturing of slaves on the "Documenting the American South" website sponsored by the University of North Carolina at Chapel Hill. Students can consider this essential question: "If runaway slave capture or even free-black capture happened in a student's backyard, what does this mean for a young nation's priorities and laws for individual rights?"

In *Chains*, Anderson quotes from Thomas Paine's *Common Sense* as an epigraph to chapter 1: "Youth is the seedtime of good habits, as well in nations as in individuals" (p. 3). A question to pose to students is, "Did the United States begin as a nation of good habits, or were there bad habits that it has struggled to end?" When considering how the content standards intersect with this text, there is an additional question that can guide student response: "How, throughout U.S. history, have African Americans and other groups been oppressed?" The overall goal, of course, is that in all things, students begin asking these questions of themselves and working toward change as citizens of their classroom, community, country, and world. This speaks to the social studies standards that require students to engage in activities intended to contribute to solving a national or international problem studied (GLCE P4.2.2).

WHILE READING *CHAINS*

Many of the activities suggested in this chapter rely both on the plot events and on the primary Revolutionary Period documents that serve as epigraphs for each of Anderson's chapters. Readers may be so involved in Anderson's captivating plot that they may skip these epigraphs in their rush to learn what happens to characters next. (In fact, we contributors did this very thing when we read the text for the first time!) Skipping these epigraphs, however, can cause readers to overlook one important value of this text: Anderson's ability to contextualize historical documents in relation to plot events, and in that effort point to the importance of the written word as a historical force.

Teachers can, and should, read each epigraph aloud with students; however, teachers should not engage in round-robin reading or send students home to read this text on their own. In fact, Albright and Ariail (2005) acknowledge the literary engagement that happens when students read texts together with the guidance of a fluent, expressive reader such as the teacher. While a teacher can indeed read the entire text aloud, please note that the audiobook of this text is particularly effective, with Madison Leigh offering an array of voices to add dimension to the novel's prose as well as each epigraph. In this way, readers can experience the text in its entirety and comprehend the text more fully in relation to the primary documents that Anderson shares.

Reading Primary Documents

Asking students to read primary documents closely relates to the standards' directive that calls for students to analyze primary documents. Teachers can use the epigraphs at the beginning of each chapter of *Chains* as an opportunity for such analysis, drawing on the aforementioned close reading strategies (Beers & Probst, 2015) in these analysis efforts. For example, chapter 5 begins with a letter written by Patrick M'Robert, which describes how "it rather hurts the European eye to see so many slaves upon the streets." In this instance, discussing M'Robert's contrasts and contradictions ("brisk and lively" vs. slaves), extreme language ("hurts"—does it mean what we think it means?) and numbers and stats (a fifth of the inhabitants of New York) can help the teacher revisit the "habits of the nation" discussion that began the novel. Such close reading strategies can be used with similar epigraphs throughout.

Students can also be encouraged to determine central ideas presented in a primary source and provide a summary of the source distinct from prior knowledge or opinions. Looking at chapter 21's epigraph, which describes the sale of slaves from the *New York Gazette*, teachers can have students consider, through a think/pair/share or journaling the following:

- In your opinion, what is the purpose of this document?
- Describe what items are for sale.
- What about this advertisement surprises you?
- What does this advertisement reveal about the habits of its society?
- Considering that Anderson has shared this particular primary document, what do you think might happen in this chapter?

Kinesthetic Engagement: Capture the Flag and the Revolutionary War

Chapters 5, 6, and 7 of the Teachers' Curriculum Institute (TCI) textbook and the series *History Alive! The United States through Industrialism* (Bower & Lobdell, 2005) can be utilized for a unique kinesthetic activity that highlights both the plight of slaves during the Revolution, while revealing causes for ultimate victory by the Americans. In this experiential activity, students participate in a game of capture the flag, playing roles as American, British, and French armies during the Revolutionary War. This activity can work at several spots in the book: in chapter 25, Isabel says, "You are blind. They don't want us free. They just want liberty for themselves" (p. 161); in chapter 33 where Curzon is captured (p. 204); or even with the epigraph that begins chapter 34 which describes the 5,000 prisoners in New York as "ragamuffins" (p. 206).

During the activity, the students designated as the Continental Army are told they will receive a prize, such as a can of soda, if they win the game of capture the flag, just like Americans would receive the prize of freedom from Great Britain. As a wrinkle, one carefully selected student is told that because he or she is a slave, the prize (can of soda) is not guaranteed. Knowing this, and in that moment, the student/slave may choose to change sides, representing the British offer of freedom for slaves who fought against Americans. The designated student may choose NOT to switch to the British cause and take chances with the American team. At the end of the activity, while the victorious American team members each receive their prize, a very deliberate point needs to be made—the designated student/slave does not receive the prize if they chose to remain on the American side.

While there are many talking points to work with throughout this activity, *Chains* provides an angle and voice to history that students may not otherwise recognize. Curzon, in an attempt to gain his freedom as a slave and American, fights for the Continental Army. It is worth noting, however, Curzon's savage treatment in jail, as he is not seen as a soldier, but as a slave (see discussion questions below for ideas on how to engage this very issue). In the end, Curzon's presumed freedom is realized only by escaping New York with Isabel.

Discussion Questions

Regardless of whether there are discussion questions before, during, or after reading *Chains*, there is value in Brian White's (1993) research on authentic—as opposed to basic comprehension—questions. Among other goals, such questions encourage students to consider an author's point of view or purpose, and draw on evidence from the text to support their analysis. White's work focuses on asking three types of questions for authentic response: prediction, author's generalization, and structural generalization. Example discussion questions for *Chains* follow:

Prediction

- In chapter 27, Isabel asks, "Would the British truly free me? Should I flee to them? What about Ruth; would they help me find her?" (p. 169) At this point in the story, what do you think she will do? Who do you feel that Isabel will trust, and why?

- When Isabel finishes reading *Common Sense* (Ch. 43, pp. 272–273), she considers her freedom. What do you think it will take for her to be free?
- *Chains* ends with Isabel and Curzon rowing a boat to Jersey. Given what you know of their choices so far, what do you think awaits them? Do you think they will remain loyal to their cause?
- Given what we know about the "habits of a nation" found in *Chains*, do you think that Isabel and Ruth will ever be reunited? Why or why not?

Author's Generalization

- Isabel is able to read. What do you think Anderson is trying to say about literacy through Isabel's skill?
- The prison conditions for Curzon are deplorable (Ch. 35, p. 221). What do you think Anderson is trying to say about prison conditions during the Revolutionary War? About the conditions of slavery during the Revolutionary War?

Structural Generalization

- Isabel's mother and father are brought up in various places throughout the story. What does this say to you about Isabel's family traditions? In your opinion, how might *Chains* have been different without mentioning Isabel's mother and father?
- Anderson uses primary documents at the beginning of each chapter, which plays a part in telling the story. In your opinion, how might this book have been different without these epigraphs (primary documents)?
- What do you feel is the most important primary document shared in this book? Why?
- Anderson chose to have Isabel as the narrator of this book. How might this book have been different if Curzon had been the narrator?

AFTER READING *CHAINS*

Given that one of the main themes of the book is Isabel's freedom from slavery, a fitting culminating activity can ask students to consider her perspective and her desire. Erin Fry and Nicole Boylan (n.d.) suggest that students play the part of Isabel and write a letter to the Continental Congress requesting, and providing reasons for, her freedom. There is also a revision to this activity; teachers have students trade these letters. Students can consider how the Continental Congress would respond by crafting a reply to Isabel. This activity is valuable for a variety of reasons: it allows students to enter Wilhelm's (2016) connective dimension, "being" the character; it considers the motivations of not only Isabel, who desires freedom, but also the Continental Congress, whose country's economic well-being relies heavily on the economy of the slave trade; it is authentic writing that allows for students to write to a "real" audience. In doing this activity, students can also demonstrate their ability to write to inform or persuade. Finally, this activity can conclude with a class discussion regarding the "habits of a nation" observed in the text as well as in these letters, and what present-day connections exist.

EXTENSION ACTIVITIES BEYOND *CHAINS*

Encourage students to revisit previous questions, discussions, and activities when studying the Civil War as well as when reading related texts such as *The Narrative of the Life of Frederick Douglass*, *Huckleberry Finn*, or *Twelve Years a Slave*. The habits of a nation, as well as the oppression of African Americans, are relevant topics when discussing the Civil Rights Movement, especially in the present day.

John Green's U.S. History Crash Course YouTube Series

John Green provides a fun, energetic summary on the important events of U.S. history. The twelve-minute videos move quickly through topics such as settlement, policy, and historical events.

Mission U.S.: Flight to Freedom Game

In this interactive, online role-playing game sponsored by New York Public Media, students take on the role of Lucy King, a fourteen-year-old runaway slave. It can be found at http://www.mission-us.org/pages/landing-mission-2.

The National Archives Pictures of the Revolutionary War

This site can help students enter the evocative dimension, visualizing the story world in *Chains*.

Liberty! The American Revolution Chronicles

Sponsored by PBS, these newspaper accounts let students "experience first hand the excitement and uncertainty of the American Revolution as it happened."

CONCLUSION

A notable value of *Chains* is that students who have engaged with its plot and characters can further engage with the entire trilogy: *Forge* (2010) follows Curzon and Isabel acting as freed slaves taking part in the Valley Forge encampment with the Patriot army; and the trilogy's final book, *Ashes* (2016), continues this journey as they search for Isabel's sister Ruth and pursue their freedom. Teachers who desire to explore content area standards as well as encourage pleasure reading can keep copies of these subsequent texts in their classroom libraries along with additional resources suggested.

Annotated List of Related YA Literature

Forge (320 pp.) and *Ashes* (304 pp.) by Laurie Halse Anderson

Completing the Seeds of America Trilogy, these novels continue to follow Isabel and Cruzon as they sort out the tangled threads of their friendship and search for Isabel's sister Ruth, while figuring out what stands between the two of them and true freedom.

King George: What Was His Problem? by Steve Sheinkin (224 pp.)

Richly illustrated, this often irreverent and humorous book shares little-known facts about the Revolutionary War. Its target audience is fourth grade through seventh, making it an excellent supplementary text for students who desire visual representations and/or accessible descriptions of the war.

Time Enough for Drums by Ann Rinaldi (256 pp.)

This coming-of-age story that takes place during the American Revolution. Sixteen-year-old Jemima Emerson and her family and strong patriots who believe in what the colonists Americans are fighting for. When the family men join the war for independence from the British king, Jemima struggles to keep things going at home.

REFERENCES

Albright, L. K., & Ariail, M. (2005). Tapping the potential of teacher read-alouds in middle schools. *Journal of Adolescent & Adult Literacy, 48*(7), 582–591.

Anderson, L. H. (2008). *Chains*. New York: Simon & Schuster Books for Young Readers.

Anderson, L. H. (2010). *Forge*. New York: Atheneum Books for Young Readers.

Anderson, L. H. (2016). *Ashes*. New York: Atheneum Books for Young Readers.

Beers, G. K., & Probst, R. E. (2015). *Reading nonfiction: Notice & note stances, signposts, and strategies*. Portsmouth, NH: Heinemann.

Bird, E. (2008, October 4). Review of the day: *Chains* by Laurie Halse Anderson. Retrieved from http://blogs.slj.com/afuse8production/2008/10/04/review-of-the-day-chains-by-laurie-halse-anderson/.

Bower, B., & Lobdell, J. (2005). *History alive!: The United States through industrialism*. Palo Alto, CA: Teachers' Curriculum Institute.

Finkelman, P. (2012, November 30). *The Monster of Monticello*. Retrieved from http://www.nytimes.com/2012/12/01/opinion/the-real-thomas-jefferson.html.

Fry, E., & Boylan, N. (n.d.). *Chains* guide (Curriculum Guide). Retrieved from http://curriculumspecialists.weebly.com/uploads/3/9/2/8/39281807/chains_tg_final.pdf.

Rinaldi, A. (2000). *Time enough for drums*. New York: Laurel Leaf.

Sheinkin, S. (2008). *King George: What was his problem?* New York: Roaring Brook Press.

Sullivan, A., & Brown, M. (2013). *Social inequalities in cognitive scores at age 16: The role of reading*. London, UK: Centre for Longitudinal Studies.

Unchained Memories: Readings from the Slave Narratives (2003). United States: HBO. Retrieved from https://youtu.be/xjjb-7R02Rw.

White, B. (1993). Pulling students toward meaning or making meaning with students: Asking authentic questions in the literature classroom. *Language Arts Journal of Michigan, 9*(1), 28–40.

Wilhelm, J. D. (2016). *You gotta BE the book: Teaching engaged and reflective reading with adolescents*. New York: Teachers College Press.

Chapter 3

Bud, Not Buddy in Social Studies: Trials and Tribulations during the Great Depression

Malinda Hoskins Lloyd and James E. Akenson

Bud, Not Buddy by Christopher Paul Curtis (1999) provides an example of how young adult (YA) literature may enhance the teaching of social studies. Set during the Great Depression, the novel addresses personal, cultural, and historical issues as a young African American male attempts to connect to family, affirm his identify, and negotiate his way through the most difficult of economic times. *Bud, Not Buddy* fits literally and metaphorically with common themes in literature such as "the road." Jones (2009) claims, "The 'road' in literature is a theme, a symbol, an organizing principle . . . every work of literature, like every road, offers up a unique journey" (par. 1). Bud's journey may be metaphorically and literally analyzed as a "journey" in historical time and physical space as Bud grapples with a wide variety of subthemes.

Physically, Bud's journey centers in the Upper Midwest and lends itself to systematic development of academic vocabulary drawn from the ten themes of social studies: Culture; Time, Continuity, and Change; People, Places, and Environments; Individual Development and Identity; Individuals, Groups, and Institutions; Power, Authority, and Governance; Production, Distribution, and Consumption; Science, Technology, and Society; Global Connections; and, Civic Ideals and Practices (NGO & CCSSO, 2010). These themes thus become significant tools in conceptualizing and locating Bud's search for identity running from Flint to Grand Rapids, Michigan. The historical context of the 1930s Great Depression emphasizing impermanence and scarcity in the context of Hoovervilles, shanty towns, race, class, and gender makes Bud's search for his family identity powerful. *Bud, Not Buddy* provides a potent narrative vehicle through which plot, point of view, and details make curricular content come alive for students in an integrated, thematic manner.

BUD, NOT BUDDY BY PAUL CHRISTOPHER CURTIS (280 PP.)

Bud, Not Buddy receives its impetus from childhood and family memories of author Christopher Paul Curtis who grew up in a stable, nuclear family. Centered in the Flint, Michigan region, Bud Caldwell begins his journey as a ten year old transitioning from an orphanage to a foster parent "temporary-care home." From the start, Bud provides a first-person point-of-view narrative of his journey from the foster parent childcare system to independent wanderer to finding his family roots. Throughout Bud's narrative journey, he lives as a second-class citizen, marginalized by race and class, set in the context of the Great Depression.

Bud first moves from an institutionalized orphanage setting to a brief foster care residency. The foster care residency lasts less than a single night. Hostile and abusive twelve-year-old Todd Amos shoves a Ticonderoga pencil up Bud's nose in a show of dominant force, and the Amos adults have obvious negative views of Bud. Bud's journey continues its impermanent nature as he experiences brief encounters with the welfare system soup lines, attempts to "ride-the-rails," and walking to Grand Rapids to find his family. Along his journey, Bud also encounters hostile Flint police who want the cardboard Hooverville shanty town destroyed and a chance encounter near Sundown Town Owosso, Michigan, that returns Bud back to Flint. The return to Flint leads to Bud meeting Herman Caldwell and others who ultimately determine his family linkage. Herman Caldwell proves to be Bud's grandfather and father to his mother, Angela Janet Caldwell.

Bud's journey manifests itself literally as he attempts to move from the Hooverville shanty town outside of Flint to Grand Rapids, Michigan, where he thinks he may find his family roots. Symbolically, Bud's suitcase is a tangible object that contains the link to his identity quest with flyers for performances, gigs by Herman E. Caldwell and His Dusky Devastators of the Depression band. The flyers, given to him by his mother prior to her death, provide Bud with an inkling of his family lineage, prod him on with a sense of purpose, and endlessly offer him hope in the quest to identify his family. The establishment of Herman Caldwell as Bud's grandfather leads to the final linkage. Bud learns to play the saxophone, determines that he will become an accomplished musician, and begins his journey to becoming a member of Herman Caldwell's Dusky Devastators. The saxophone consequently becomes the tangible, symbolic link to Bud's family and future just as the flyers served to be the symbolic, tangible link to his past. Bud's journey to find his family thus becomes complete within the novel, yet points to a continued journey as a member of the Caldwell family and extended family of Dusky Devastator musicians. *Bud, Not Buddy* therefore answers "no" to the eternal question, "Will the circle be unbroken?"

CONNECTING SOCIAL STUDIES AND LITERACY

The themes within *Bud, Not Buddy* directly correlate to specific state social studies standards as well as to standards of the National Council for the Social Studies (NCSS). Specifically, *Bud, Not Buddy* and the era of the 1930s Great Depression fit with the statement by NCSS,

> The primary purpose of social studies is to help young people make informed and reasoned decisions for the public good as citizens of a culturally diverse, democratic society in an interdependent world.
>
> (NCSS, 2010, p. 3)

Bud, Not Buddy has the potential to engage students, through literature, to become familiar with the zeitgeist of the era, the overall spirit of the time period, and, in particular, the Great Depression (Harris, 2010). Harris defines the "zeitgeist of an era" as "the historical theme or set of themes that the populace perceived at that time or the historical perspective we now have regarding the themes, intellectual trend and tone of an historical period of movement" (p. 17). Using the Comprehension Windows Strategy (CWS) by Bass and Woo (2008) as a premise for a zeitgeist reading and writing project, students can explore the parallels between the events in the novel and the nonfiction accounts from the primary sources provided as part of the text set (refer to the post-reading activities and the annotated bibliography). As a support for this culminating activity, the authors have provided scaffolded activities throughout the study of the novel to help students synthesize historical research with a literary analysis of *Bud, Not Buddy*.

Integrated Strategies for Bridging Theory to Practice

Bud, Not Buddy contains history-related topics such as the crash of the stock market, Hooverville, racism, sundown towns, and, particularly, life during the Great Depression. This Newbery and Coretta Scott King award-winning novel is suitable for middle-grade learners; however, due to its inclusion of in-depth concepts, the novel is also applicable for higher grade levels. In addition, these activities could be adapted for diverse learners in grades six through twelve.

Relying heavily on Samuels and Farstrup's (2011) *What Research Has to Say about Reading Instruction* as the foundation, the authors provide suggested best practices to assist teachers in connecting theory to practice in the history classroom. In addition, the information presented is based on the Scaffolded Reading Experience (SRE), an instructional framework which includes a set of pre-, during-, and post-reading strategies designed to enhance students' comprehension of various texts (Graves & Fitzgerald, 2009); however, teachers may choose to implement the activities at various entry points throughout their lessons.

BEFORE READING *BUD, NOT BUDDY*

Pre-reading strategies are used to motivate students, relate the reading to their lives, and to pre-teach concepts or vocabulary. As you prepare students to engage in a reading of *Bud, Not Buddy,* it is also important to provide students with background context as a means of activating their schema. The following activities are suggested to serve this purpose.

Critical Thinking and the Facilitate-Listen-Engage (FLE) Model

Fostering critical thinking and engaging students in discourse play a central role in deepening student learning. Lloyd, Kolodziej, and Brashears (2016) encourage the implementation of the FLE model, a framework for promoting "horizontal" discourse which is representative of rich student-student and student-teacher interactions and establishes a sense of community in the classroom. In this context, students' voices are valued as they engage in a reciprocal exchange of ideas with the teacher and their peers. To do this, teachers plan activities that spark critical thinking and purposely engage students in literacy-related conversations. One way of implementing this framework for *Bud, Not Buddy* is to introduce students to the harsh conditions of the 1930s through photographs from the era (*Washington Post*, 2015) that convey events or themes such as the Dust Bowl and racism and having them critically analyze the images. Have students partner or discuss in small groups to foster active discussions, noting particular evidence of the marginalization of African Americans. These pictures can build students' background knowledge and generate lively discourse with respect to the primary themes within the novel.

Semantic Maps

Teachers can also utilize a semantic map as a means of activating students' background knowledge. For this activity, students write what they already know, or believe they know, about the Great Depression on a post-it note. The teacher can then create a semantic map by writing "The Great Depression" on a chart. Based on students' responses on the post-it notes, the teacher and the students will create categories—who was involved, where did this occur, when did this happen, what other words contain the base word "depress," what were the key causes, what were the effects—and organize their responses according to the categories on the semantic map. This type of activity requires students to make connections with words and concepts.

Analyzing Music Lyrics

Another way to activate students' schema or pique their interest prior to reading is to play a song from the era such as "We're in the Money" (Warren & Dubin, 1933) and provide students with a copy of the lyrics. Students highlight key words and phrases in the lyrics that they believe are related to the Great Depression. In the left margin, students make a predicted analysis of the meaning of the highlighted information. For example, students could highlight the words, "The long lost dollar has come back to the fold" or "We never see a headline 'bout a breadline today" and write in the left margin their predicted analysis of the words. At the end of the novel study, or as they gather information along the way, students can write their revised analyses in the right-hand margin based on the knowledge they have gained.

Project-Based Learning (PBL)

Research shows PBL motivates students, deepens learning, and parallels the skills needed in the workplace and college settings, while engaging students in a constructive investigation (Thomas, 2000). To design a PBL activity, the teacher crafts a problem for which students engage in inquiry to arrive at a solution. A suggested PBL project could have students working in small groups to create an imaginary scenario for locating a friend or relative with whom they have lost contact. They could generate a list of steps for finding this person. Connecting this to *Bud, Not Buddy*, students could compare and contrast their course of action with Bud's strategies for finding his father. Students may also choose to take a more contemporary approach by exploring technological advances to extend their search. For example, students may implore the use of cell phones, iPads, a GPS, a digital application (an app), or any other digital device they can justify as useful for locating a distant relative or lost loved one. Based on this approach, students could extend this activity by developing a timeline of technological advances ranging from the Depression era to today. Further, students could be presented with another project-based learning activity in which they designate the best route for Bud to take for his travels using modern-day technology devices and/or apps.

WHILE READING *BUD, NOT BUDDY*

Employing strategies while reading helps students to remain engaged and helps them monitor their comprehension and make adjustments as needed. Throughout the reading of the novel, students engage in activities such as exploring literary devices (characterization, foreshadowing, imagery, mood, theme, and symbolism). Teachers engage students in discourse, ask higher-order questions, and provide supports and tools including graphic organizers, anchor charts, and other visuals. Below are some activities that serve this purpose.

Graphic and Semantic Organizers

Graphic and semantic organizers are one of the eight effective strategies supported by the National Reading Panel to increase reading comprehension (Fautsch-Partridge, McMaster, & Hupp, 2011). One strategy that can be employed using a graphic organizer is the use of a word web. For example, the word *depress* could be explored by having students analyze its relationship to words such as tropical depression, depressed, and the Great Depression. Another idea for utilizing a word web is to have students explore the words sentimental, cynical, sarcastic, welcoming, discouraging, threatening, and caustic by writing the word, a definition in their own words, a synonym, and an antonym. Then ask them to circle the words that describe the Owasso sign that says "Negro Friends." Have them explain reasons for circling the chosen words.

Another graphic organizer that can be utilized while reading *Bud, Not Buddy* is a tri-chart (an organizer with three columns). Have students write statements that indicate people were prejudiced against African Americans in the first column (pp. 205–206). In the second column, students draw pictures of items mentioned on these pages that would be declared unconstitutional today. In the third column, students write the statement or amendment in the Constitution that specifically relates to this. Have students use technology as needed.

Integration of Story Elements and Geography

According to research, good readers are cognizant of the characters and settings of texts (Duke, Pearson, Strachan, & Billman, 2011); therefore, students should engage in activities which emphasize story elements. To promote this, students are given a map of the United States. Using the five themes of geography (region, movement, human-land interaction, location, and place) to further understand Bud's experiences and the development of his character, students plot the Midwest, specifically the two cities of Chicago and Flint that are mentioned (p. 57). Students outline these two states and then locate the exact grid coordinates for Flint. Students then locate the region of Michigan in which the events take place and mark this area with crosshatching. Focusing on this region, ask students to react to the following quotation: "To Our Negro Friends Who Are Passing Through, Kindly Don't Let the Sun Set on

Your Rear End in Owosso!" (p. 105) Although Owosso, Michigan, is in the Midwest, prompt students to discuss what makes it so dangerous for Bud. Based on Bud's visits to these areas, have students discuss racism and support their claims with text-based evidence. Engage students in discourse by having them turn to a shoulder partner and explain the meaning of the phrase "sundown town" and its relation to racism.

AFTER READING *BUD, NOT BUDDY*

Post-reading strategies serve as a catalyst for providing opportunities for students to respond to texts, recall important information, and synthesize and organize information (Graves & Graves, 2003). We have included one culminating post-reading activity; however, many of the activities listed, including the extension activities, could be implemented as post-reading activities.

Comprehension Windows Strategy (CWS)

Bass and Woo's CWS (2008) is an interactive organizer used as a tool for engaging students in citing text-based evidence and integrating reading and writing in multiple content areas. Using a text set related to *Bud, Not Buddy*, students locate and organize text-based evidence structured around specific headings as they gather information for a writing piece. This strategy introduces students to proper procedures for citing sources. When designing the CWS, some teachers prefer to provide the headings for which students will gather information, while others design the activity as a more open-ended project, allowing the students to develop their own headings. We have provided suggested headings for the CWS using *Bud, Not Buddy* along with extension activities which correlate with the headings. What follows is a suggested culminating activity based on the Comprehension Windows Strategy.

Students complete a zeitgeist reading and writing project. During this activity, students use a predetermined text set and additional online sources related to *Bud, Not Buddy* to research various aspects of the Great Depression, synthesizing their knowledge of the major concepts. The students compile their findings and are given a choice of a finished product: creating a brochure using pages (application on a Mac), constructing a newspaper article, or writing a script for and dramatizing a talk show or live news report. This final product should contain a compilation of text-based evidence with citations to represent their understandings of the following concepts: What evidence, artifacts, and events depict unsafe or discriminative conditions for African Americans during the 1930s? What were the causes and effects of the Great Depression? What were the results of Franklin D. Roosevelt's New Deal?

TECHNOLOGY-INTEGRATED EXTENSION ACTIVITIES
BEYOND *BUD, NOT BUDDY*

Extension activities provide a backdrop for differentiating instruction or simply extending the reading of the novel. With the influx of social media and multiple technologies, media literacy is paramount in today's classroom. Blanchard and Farstrup (2011) argue that technology and digital media are avid components of children's and teachers' daily lives and can be used as motivational tools for active learning. In the activities that follow, students are encouraged to use some form(s) of technology to locate information.

Based on the ten themes of social studies delineated by NCSS, have students create a fictional Instagram, SnapChat, or Facebook post that portrays Bud's experiences with respect to each of these themes. Pose the following prompt: If he had access to these forms of social media during the era in which the novel is set, what might he have posted?

In *Bud, Not Buddy*, Curtis makes numerous references to crime. Using a personal device, locate the following individuals mentioned in the text: John Dillinger (p. 17), Pretty Boy Floyd (p. 37), Baby Face Nelson (p. 106), Machine Gun Kelly (p. 133), and Al Capone (p. 136). How do crimes prevalent in today's news compare to crime in the 1930s? Enlist a group of four-five classmates to create a script from a live news report in the 1930s and one from today. How do they differ? How are they alike?

With a partner, use the text and a personal device to explore Blind Lemon Jefferson (p. 164). Create a diagram of the influence of Jefferson on diverse people such as B. B. King, Bob Dylan, the Beatles, and Carl Perkins. Be prepared to explain how your diagram reflects diversity in U.S. culture. Next, explore another world-famous musician from the 1930s, Paul Robeson (p. 29) on your personal device. Of the two (Jefferson or Robeson), which one would probably be appreciated the most by Kanye West, Drake, Fortune, the Rolling Stones, the Avett Brothers, Bob Dylan, the Beatles, and Jack White? Imagine the two famous musicians from the 1930s talking with the others mentioned here. Write the script for or simulate an interview which might have occurred if these musicians had met each other.

Herman E. Calloway navigated his way through racial prejudice with courage and resilience. On p. 205, locate the statement that shows how he managed to book his bands at venues without Whites knowing they were African Americans until they arrived. What musical styles did Herman E. Calloway and his bands play that were unlike the jazz or swing of the 1930s? Discuss these points with a partner. Next, using technology explore and listen to examples of "oom pah-pah" and polka music, which are referenced in the novel. What does this tell you about the ethnic origins of many people in Michigan in the 1930s?

The role of women throughout history has evolved. Use a personal device to further explore Dorothy Dandridge (p. 112) with respect to women's roles in American society. Prepare two imaginary interviews with Ms. Dandridge, one in the 1930s and one from today. Enlist the help of a partner with one person being the interviewer and one the interviewee. Be prepared to perform the interview for your classmates. Provide evidence of how women's roles have evolved since the 1930s.

Introduce students to these websites and have them cite three interesting facts from each, creating a fact page of twelve items to stimulate interest in other topics.

- Website for Christopher Paul Curtis at http://www.nobodybutcurtis.com/
- Library of Congress Primary Source Sets on The Great Depression at http://www.loc.gov/teachers/classroommaterials/themes/great-depression/set.html
- The Gilder Lehrman Institute of American History: Information on The Great Depression at https://www.gilderlehrman.org/history-by-era/great-depression-and-world-war-ii-1929-1945/great-depression
- Everyday Life During the Great Depression at http://depts.washington.edu/depress/everyday_life.shtml

Students will become highly engaged in exploring, so don't be surprised if students spend a lot of time doing this extension activity.

CONCLUSION

Bud, Not Buddy clearly lends itself to the standards in the social studies, requiring the development of academic vocabulary and higher-order thinking. Young adult literature provides avenues for engagement and involvement with deep, substantive content. The integration of adolescent literature in the content areas contributes to understanding and exploration beyond the confines of standard texts and promises to enrich, elaborate, and create students' depth of understanding.

Annotated List of Related YA Literature

Stella by Starlight by Sharon Draper (362 pp.)

When a burning cross set by the Klu Klux Klan causes panic and fear in 1932 Bumblebee, North Carolina, fifth-grader Stella must face prejudice and find the strength to demand change in her segregated town.

Out of the Dust by Karen Hesse (240 pp.)

This 1998 Newbery-winning text is written in first person, free verse and is narrated by fourteen-year-old Billie Jo during the 1930s Dust Bowl and the Great Depression. Billie Jo faces numerous hardships: losing her mother, living with her grieving father, and suffering a tragic injury that temporarily ends her ability to play her beloved piano.

Roll of Thunder, Hear My Cry by Mildred Taylor (288 pp.)

This Newbery award-winner is set in southern Mississippi during the Great Depression. The main character, Cassie Logan, is African American who learns firsthand about the ruthless effects of racism and social injustice. Over the course of a year, she also learns the importance of her family's fight to rightfully keep their land and their dignity.

REFERENCES

Bass, M. L., & Woo, D. G. (2008). Comprehension windows strategy: A comprehension strategy and prop for reading and writing informational text. *The Reading Teacher, 61*(7), 571–575.

Blanchard, J. S., & Farstrup, A. E. (2011). Technologies, digital media, and reading instruction. In S. J. Samuels & A. E. Farstrup (Eds.), *What research has to say about reading instruction*. Newark, DE: International Reading Association.

Curtis, C. P. (1999). *Bud, not buddy*. New York: Dell Yearling.

Draper, S. (2016). *Stella by starlight*. New York: Atheneum/Caitlyn Dlouhy Books.

Duke, N. K., Pearson, P. D., Strachan, S. L., & Billman, A. K. (2011). Essential elements of fostering and teaching reading comprehension. In S. J. Samuels & A. E. Farstrup (Eds.), *What research has to say about reading instruction*. Newark, DE: International Reading Association.

Fautsch-Partridge, T., McMaster, K. L., & Hupp, S. C. (2011). Are current reading research findings applicable to students with intellectual disabilities? In S. J. Samuels & A. E. Farstrup (Eds.), *What research has to say about reading instruction*. Newark, DE: International Reading Association.

Graves, M. F., & Fitzgerald, J. (2009). Implementing scaffolded reading experiences in diverse classrooms. In J. Coppola & E. Primas (Eds.), *One classroom, many learners: Best literacy practices for today's multilingual classrooms*, 119–139. Newark, DE: International Reading Association.

Graves, M. F., & Graves, B. B. (2003). *Scaffolded reading experiences: Designs for student success* (2nd ed.). Norwood, MA: Christopher-Gordon.

Harris, J. (2010). Our zeitgeist: Fighting the white noise. In *Engaging students with literature: A curriculum module for AP English literature and composition*, 14–31. New York: The College Board.

Hesse, K. (1997). *Out of the dust*. New York: Scholastic.

Jones, A. (2009). *Word search with Adair Jones*. Retrieved from https://adairjones.wordpress.com/2009/07/13/in-search-of-the-road-in-literature/.

Lloyd, M., Kolodziej, N., & Brashears, K. (2016). The Facilitate, Listen, Engage (FLE) model: Strategies to promote community through classroom discourse. *School Community Journal, 26*(2), 291–304.

National Council for the Social Studies (NCSS) (2010). *National curriculum standards for social studies: A framework for teaching, learning, and assessment.* Silver Spring, MD.

National Governors Association Center for Best Practices (NGA) & Council of Chief State School Officers (CCSSO) (2010). *Common core state standards for English language arts and literacy in history/social studies, science, and technical subjects.* Washington, DC: Authors.

Samuels, S. J., & Farstrup, A. E. (2011). *What research has to say about reading instruction* (4th ed.). Newark, DE: International Reading Association.

Taylor, M. D. (1976). *Roll of thunder, hear my cry*. New York: Puffin Publishing.

Thomas, J. W. (2000). *A review of research on project-based learning*. San Rafael, CA: Autodesk Foundation.

Warren, H., & Dubin, A. (1933). We're in the money. *The Gold Diggers Song.* 42nd Street Original Broadway Cast recording. Thomas Z. Sheppard.

Washington Post (2015, November 13). *Stunning photos show what America looked like during the Great Depression*. Retrieved from www.washingtonpost.com/news/wonk/wp/2015/11/13/what-america-looked-like-during-the-great-depression/.

Chapter 4

Using *The Storm in the Barn* to Study the Dust Bowl: Comics as Triggers for Inquiry

Crag Hill and Kristy A. Brugar

It is not surprising to most secondary English language arts (ELA) and history teachers that inside and outside of the classroom, comics and graphic novels have become increasingly popular. Once Art Spiegleman's *Maus* (2003) was awarded the Pulitzer Prize in 1992 and then *Persepolis* (Satrapi, 2004), *American Born Chinese* (Yang, 2006), and *The March Trilogy* (Lewis, 2016) were awarded the National Book Award, many other graphic novels have become staples in secondary curriculum across the country. Comics have been used to supplement disciplinary content, as a bridge to more complex texts for English Language Learners (ELLs) and other readers who struggle with assigned texts, and simply as a way to expand the choices students have in their independent reading. In fact, Carter (2007) has argued "there is a graphic novel for virtually every learner" (p. 1). We have also realized comics and graphic novels are opportunities to promote inter/disciplinary literacy practices as well as critical literacy with adolescents in ELA and history classrooms. For this chapter, we define *comics* as a literary form that utilizes sequential art to tell a story with verbal (printed words) and nonverbal (illustrations) elements within bounded panels (McCloud, 1994; Versaci, 2007). *Graphic novels* are book-length narratives, either fiction or nonfiction, that are written in the comics medium.

Graphic novels are intricately told stories in which the reader must negotiate words and images, often containing symbolism (Carter, 2007; McCloud, 1994; Versaci, 2007). Not every reader is knowledgeable about how to read this kind of complicated text (Jimenez & Meyer, 2016). This is particularly true among graphic novels commonly used in history classes including Spiegleman's *Maus*, Satrapi's *Persepolis*, and Hale's *Nathan Hale's Hazardous Tales*. Thus, literacy and history curriculum and instruction work in tandem in meaningful and supportive ways.

From a history perspective, as teachers and students read they draw from multiple resources (including prior knowledge), discuss the validity and reliability of evidence, and enable students to practice sourcing information by utilizing primary sources and only employing texts that contain references. In order to explore these disciplinary literacy skills, we designed a lesson in which students studying twentieth-century history, particularly The Dust Bowl, read an excerpt from *The Storm in the Barn* (Phelan, 2011) and begin to model and develop aspects of the "inquiry arc" outlined in *The College, Career, and Civic Life (C3) Framework* (National Council for the Social Studies, 2013).

THE STORM IN THE BARN BY MATT PHELAN (208 PP.)

When *The Storm in the Barn* begins, the dust has already wreaked havoc on the Great Plains region of the United States. Families are packing up and abandoning their farms. But something else is awry. On the way out of town in a blinding dust storm, one family almost hits something on the road, a strange apparition the father cannot identify and then discounts as a figment of the storm.

The main character, eleven-year-old Jack who's bullied by the older boys in the community, would like to help his father Tom on the farm, but there is no such work to be done; the farm's topsoil has been eroded by winds and drought. When Jack is almost caught in a gargantuan dust storm on his way home from town, Jack's parents are wracked with fear. Desperate to protect him from falling sick to the omnipresent dust—his sister is already bedbound, prone to crippling coughing attacks—his parents decide to leave as soon as the father can fix the car.

One night, Jack witnesses a flash of light coming from the barn on the abandoned neighboring farm, which he at first thinks might be a symptom of dust dementia, a term he overheard the doctor use. With nothing to keep him occupied, Jack's curiosity eventually spurs him to investigate. Over the next few days, what Jack encounters and how he confronts what he has discovered changes his life and the lives of others. Jack's bold actions lead to the promise of renewal for the community, and Jack, an unwitting hero, will never be underestimated again.

BEFORE READING *THE STORM IN THE BARN*

Using Visual Thinking Strategies (VTS) to Engage Students

In order to increase comprehension, build text-specific knowledge, and tap prior knowledge, it is critical to engage students in pre-reading exercises

(Beers, 2003). In this lesson, students' pre-reading experiences engage and scaffold the initial aspects of the inquiry arc. Using VTS (Yenawine, 2013) in which students are actively engaging with art, display a panel from *Storm in the Barn* (p. 240) (see figure 4.1). First, ask students, "What do you see?" Independently, students view the comic panel and jot notes on what they infer from reading the panel before sharing with the whole class. Encourage students to take these notes on the panel; knowing that notes appear on the back of the panel each student receives, along the margins of the images, as well as within the panel. This is an opportunity for students to make concrete observations. For example, students might remark, there are "two ladies wearing hats," or "a man wearing a lab coat," and "wearing sanitary material—mask, gloves, and glasses." Among the responses, students often note "who" is pictured in the panel provided.

In addition, students may note the actions or what is happening in the panel, noting how the author manipulates time within the panel to create tension. One student might notice that "all are looking at the same point." While several others describe "hurried motion" and identify the "swoosh" the man's hand is making, specifically noting the "motion lines" Phelan includes in the panel. Some students may begin to develop a narrative around the comic panel and hypothesize that the three figures are moving into a "quarantined zone."

Once students have exhausted their observations, as a class move on to the second of three questions associated with VTS: What story do you think the artist is trying to tell? Ask students to first discuss this question with their tablemates, encouraging them to use evidence in responding to this question. For example, one student might say, "I think there is a danger to the people so they are covered." Another might share ideas of quarantines, medical

Figure 4.1. Sample VTS Display Panel

experiments, or a general sense of menace since the reader, and arguably the other characters in the story, are unable to see the eyes and faces of these three individuals. Throughout these small group discussions, have students point to elements of the panel as they share their hypotheses. After about five minutes, students then share with the whole group the stories that emerged from their small group discussion.

Finally, ask students, "What else would you like to know about this image?" Students questions may range from the concrete (why are they wearing the masks?) to the abstract (How is the guy in the middle different?) Is he [the central figure] posh (draws attention to his dress) to the historically relevant (what is the time period? Why does the middle guy look like Hitler?) and to the generally curious (how do you fit three people in one doorway?). As students share their questions and inquiries, recorded them on a whiteboard. These student-generated questions start the inquiry process (e.g., inquiry-based questions and planning investigations, D1; explain how a question represents key ideas in the field, evaluate various sources, D1.His.1.6–8; and use other historical sources to infer a plausible maker, date, place of origin, and intended audience for historical sources where this information is not easily identified, D2.His.11.6–8) and will be used in the remainder of the lesson.

WHILE READING *THE STORM IN THE BARN*

Readers' Theater

Students' observations solicited during the pre-reading activity should pique their curiosity and generate personal connections with the text. Students will want to read more to discover "the answer" or to find out more. As a whole group, read pp. 24–29 using a reader's theater approach (Farris, 2015; Sanacore & Palumbo, 2010). This passage begins with the panel explored in the pre-reading activity, and the additional panels reveal some information about the "who," "what, and "why" of the first panel. As you read these panels and pages, make references back to the student-generated questions. Periodically ask, "Based on these panels, have any of your questions been answered?" By this time, students ought to be able to acknowledge that some questions were answered. Next ask, "Have the gathered data from these panels helped to answer these questions?"

For our purposes, this second question was more important. Students participating in the inquiry arc are not looking for "one right answer," rather they are gathering evidence to formulate one possible conclusion among many. Case in point, a student-generated question was, "Why are they wearing masks?" Based on the class reading, students were able to identify that the characters were wearing masks "to prevent them from inhaling dust." Not all questions were answered; some were in fact complicated by the additional information. The question of whether the characters were entering or exiting the room/building was of interest to the students. After reading the additional panels and pages, this question was complicated through student discussion. They started to articulate reasons for believing the three characters were moving into or out of a room. And further, several students talked about why they were entering/exiting as well as other characters that may be involved in scene but invisible to the reader. Based on the reading, students referenced a later panel in which a young boy is pulled into the house and out of the dust storm as evidence these characters were inside.

Later in the book, ask students to sketch panels of scenes they would like to have seen in the novel, especially scenes that would have helped give them the kind of information to answer their questions. In addition, ask students to create three- to five-minute videos based on the novel. Ask them to incorporate appropriate costuming, create props accurate to the time era, and add sound effects and background music to enhance the ambience of the scene or scenes they are depicting. They may create new scenes but they must be prepared to give a rationale for including them.

AFTER READING *THE STORM IN THE BARN*

Following the short During Reading activity and rich discussion, organize students into small groups to explore primary source materials associated with the Dust Bowl. The Library of Congress (n.d.) has a student discovery set that is particularly useful for this purpose, including newspaper articles, photographs, and sound recordings. As they explore these materials, encourage them to look for information associated with one or more of the questions that have been generated, to look for information between texts. These can be the questions that were displayed on the board or those they recorded but did not share with the group. Next, ask students to record the question they were exploring, the resource that was most helpful to them learning more about that question, and most importantly what new questions emerged as a result of this inquiry.

As students explored the medical issues associated with the Dust Bowl, for example, they found information about dust pneumonia in *Years of Dust* (Marrin, 2009). Our students found that the dust, particularly "Oklahoma red" dust, made people nauseous and people covered their faces with wet rags to prevent breathing in the dust as they slept. Learning that these storms went on for a long time, our students were curious if people left to avoid the dust and, if they left, where did they go? They were able to explore these questions about "Dust Bowl refugees" in *Children of the Great Depression* (Freedman, 2005).

EXTENSION ACTIVITIES BEYOND *THE STORM IN THE BARN*

We envision three possible extensions for this lesson/experience for students. First as part of this lesson, students model the inquiry process in which one develops questions and begins to investigate those questions which lead to the development of more questions. We want them to become curious about history and the world around them. We know that one way in which students finds answers to their questions is through books or other print resources. In addition, these experiences prepare students to seek answers from others through interviews. Thus, one extension could be an Author Outreach experience. In order to do this we would arrange a Skype session with the author or illustrator to answer student-generated questions. We have conducted such a session with Matt Phelan via Skype and a group of secondary ELA and social studies teacher candidates. After our teacher candidates read the whole book, as opposed to the excerpt we read with the middle school students, they interviewed Phelan around these questions:

- Did you pull the imagery of the rain king from any particular folklore?
- Why those scenes from The Wizard of Oz? Is there a particular point you were trying to make with those particular scenes?
- On pp. 128 and 145 and other pages there are boxes of color, specifically with colors of orange and red. Do the colors represent emotions? What makes you choose to use color or more neutral colors for other scenes? What is the role of color in your graphic novel? When thinking of specific colors, do you have specific meanings assigned to each color?
- What was your process in organizing the story? Did you have a storyboard or did you do use technology?
- Why did you decide to tell your story in color rather than in black and white? How did you decide when to use color and when to use duller colors?
- Do you feel like pictures tell the story of the Dust Bowl better than words?
- How long did it take you to do all the illustrations?
- What do your different art styles reflect?
- Has anyone approached you about making a movie adaptation of your work?

These questions reflected issues of authorship as well as historical content and the use of historical evidence. A second extension to secondary students' experience with *Storm in the Barn* is to ask them to read Phelan's *Snow White* (2016). This text is set at the same historical time period as *Storm in the Barn*, but instead, takes place in New York City as opposed to rural Kansas. Thus, *Snow White* may serve as an urban counternarrative and encourage students to view history through multiple perspectives. With that in mind, students complete a Venn diagram or a compare/contrast table on the two novels.

Another possible extension is to research and report out the actions the government took once it realized the magnitude of this environmental disaster. For instance, the government only got involved when dust began to blanket New York City after which they sent a group of scientists to investigate and propose ways to stem and then begin to prepare the damage. The research could include reading newspapers from the time (Egan, 2006).

CONCLUSION

This aforementioned lessons draw on language referencing history and the social sciences and *The C3 Framework* (NCSS, 2013). Discipline-specific literacy is an important component to the *C3 Framework* (National Council for the Social Studies, 2013). *The C3 Framework* focus is the *inquiry arc*, whereby students' engage in knowledge creation; thus, several standards that we reference throughout this chapter.

Annotated List of Related YA Literature

Children of the Great Depression by Russell Freedman, R. (128 pp.)

Freedman tells the stories of children representing a diversity of perspectives using their voices as well as iconic photographs of the time (e.g., The Migrant Mother), which provides greater context for this era in United States history.

Out of the Dust by Karen Hess (240 pp.)

This novel in verse tells the story of Billy Jo whose family was hit hard by fire and dust during the 1930s. Despite more than her share of tragedy, Billy Jo holds on to a glimmer of hope at the end of the novel.

Years of Dust: The Story of the Dust Bowl by Albert Marrin (144 pp.)

Marrin explores the causes and consequences of the Dust Bowl. First-person accounts and photographs are woven throughout the text.

Children of the Dust Bowl: The True Story of the School at Weedpatch Camp by Jerry Stanley (85 pp.)

This nonfiction book documents the experiences of students and teachers at a "federal emergency school" during the Great Depression.

REFERENCES

Beers (2003). *When kids can't read, what teachers can do.* Portsmouth, NH: Heinemann.

Carter, J. B. (2005). *Building literacy connections with graphic novels: Page by page, panel by panel.* Urbana, IL: National Council of Teachers of English.

Egan, T. (2006). *The worst hard time: The untold story of those who survived the great American dust bowl.* New York: Mariner Books.

Farris, P. J. (2015). *Elementary and middle school social studies: An interdisciplinary, multicultural approach.* Long Grove, IL: Waveland Press.

Freedman, R. (2005). *Children of the great depression.* New York: HMH Books for Young Readers.

Hess, K. (1997). *Out of the dust.* New York: Scholastic.

Jimenez, L. M., & Meyer, C. K. (2016). Navigating graphic novels utilizing linguistic, visual, and spatial resources. *Journal of Literacy Research, 48*(4), 423–447.

Lewis, J., Aydin, A. & Powell, N. (2016). *The march trilogy.* Marietta, GA: Top Shelf Productions.

Library of Congress (n.d.). *The dust bowl: Student discovery set.* Washington, DC: The Library of Congress.

Marrin, A. (2009). *Years of dust: The story of the dust bowl.* New York: Dutton Books for Young Readers.

McCloud, S. (1994). *Understanding comics: The invisible art.* New York: William Morrow Paperbacks.

National Council for the Social Studies (NCSS) (2013). *The college, career, and civic life (C3) framework for social studies state standards: Guidance for enhancing the rigor of K-12 civics, economics, geography, and history.* Silver Spring, MD: NCSS.

Phelan, M. (2011). *Storm in the barn.* Somerville, MA: Candlewick Press.

Phelan, M. (2016). *Snow white.* Somerville, MA: Candlewick Press.

Sanacore, J., & Palumbo, A. (2010). Middle school students need more opportunities to read across the curriculum. *The Clearing House, 83*(5), 180–185.

Satrapi, M. (2004). *Persepolis: The story of a childhood.* New York: Pantheon.

Spiegelman, A. (2003). *The complete maus.* New York: Pantheon.

Stanley, J. (1993). *Children of the dust bowl: The true story of the school at Weedpatch camp.* Danvers, MA: Crown Publishers.

Versaci, R. (2007). *This book contains graphic language: Comics as literature.* New York: Continuum.

Yang, G. L. (2006). *American born Chinese.* New York: First Second Books.

Yenawine, P. (2013). *Visual thinking strategies: Using art to deepen learning across school disciplines.* Cambridge, MA: Harvard Education Press.

Chapter 5

Understanding of the Role of Leningrad in World War II through M. T. Anderson's *Symphony for the City of the Dead: Dmitri Shostakovich and the Siege of Leningrad*

Steven T. Bickmore and Paul E. Binford

Due to years of experience in the classroom, both contributors can point to moments when a more collaborative unit of study between social studies and English language arts (ELA) would have provided students a deeper engagement with the topic being discussed. New standards have reinforced the notion that all teachers should include more informational texts and cross-curricular exchanges. This chapter explains how using an award-winning young adult (YA) nonfiction text, M. T. Anderson's *Symphony for the City of the Dead: Dmitri Shostakovich and the Siege of Leningrad* (2015) can produce a rich, social studies unit featuring one of Russia's most difficult episodes in World War II, the siege of Leningrad. As a result, we provide a discussion that models a unit that harmoniously combines the standards from both social studies and the English language arts (ELA).

Both literature and history have a place in the school curriculum, in part, because they speak to the human experience. History provides a sense of perspective through narrative content that documents continuity and change over time. It is through this historical contextualization that we can both understand and evaluate current developments. Through this knowledge of the past, we avoid distorting reality as poignantly told in the Indian fable, *The Blind Men and the Elephant* (Saxe, 2005), where each blind man's incomplete examination of the pachyderm led to six separate and inaccurate conclusions. History helps us escape the fate of these men, who—as John Godfrey Saxe has lyricized—"[were] each . . . partly in the right, [but] . . . all were in the wrong."

SYMPHONY FOR THE CITY OF THE DEAD: DMITRI
SHOSTAKOVICH AND THE SIEGE OF LENINGRAD
BY M. T. ANDERSON (464 PP.)

In *Symphony*, M. T. Anderson writes about one of the most horrific chapters in world history. The setting for Anderson's account is the siege of Leningrad both prior to and with the arrival of the Wehrmacht, the Nazi Germany war machine, in 1941. Remarkably, however, the author tells this apocalyptic account through the biography of a Russian prodigy—a composer named Dmitri Shostakovich and the music he produced in and for his native city. A quick survey of the text of *Symphony* shows that Anderson has built the book on a rich trove of primary documents, historical texts, and photographs, which add to the reader's understanding of Leningrad during World War II. Adolescents deserve texts composed with the level of engagement, care, and intellect that Anderson provides.

CONNECTING HISTORY AND LITERACY

While teaching an acclaimed nonfiction literary text like *Symphony*, a teacher could easily touch on most of the ELA standards. We choose to point to only a few in order to maintain a focus on those standards connected to social studies. As an English teacher, Steve frequently taught novels where an understanding of the historical setting is key to the tone, mood, and character conflicts within the narrative. Understanding the urge to volunteer after the bombing of Pearl Harbor provides the reader additional clarity about Finny's motives in *A Separate Peace* (Knowles, 2000). Capturing the poverty of depression era Alabama gives added insight to family situations in *To Kill a Mockingbird* (Lee, 1960). Images of the dust bowl heighten our understanding of *Out of the Dust* (Hesse, 1997). Teachers can incorporate several strategies that might be used to examine first person accounts, newspapers, and any number of informational texts to add depth to any curriculum unit.

The historian, Barbara Tuchman, observed that biography is "a prism of history" (1981, p. 81). *Symphony* refracts these broader events, so students see the vivid shades of red brought on by the senseless carnage of the Stalinist purges and Hitler's invasion. Paradoxically, however, this biography—in the midst of cataclysmic events—also reveals the delicate violet light of individual inspiration, creativity, and endurance through the life of Shostakovich and his fellow Leningrad survivors.

The deliberate distortions of Stalin's Soviet Union during the 1930s provide the political backdrop for Dmitri Shostakovich's young adult years while living in his beloved city. Psychiatrist M. Scott Peck described evil as "unreality," which aptly characterizes Josef Stalin's rule in the Soviet Union as he perpetuated a cult of personality, fabricated his Five-Year Plan's successes, and pathologically purged perceived opposition.

In *World History: Connections to Today*, Ellis and Esler (2005) briefly describe Stalin's deliberate efforts to increase confidence in communism through faith in his personage: "Stalin tried to boost morale and faith in the communist system by making himself a godlike figure. . . . This 'cult of personality' was one more pillar to support Stalin's absolute power" (p. 713).

Symphony amplifies and illustrates this glorification of Stalin. The book highlights mass rallies celebrating Stalin, including a throng of athletes marching through the streets of Moscow and "carrying portraits of Communist Party leaders, as they once carried painted icons of saints on religious holidays . . . [as p]lanes spelled out his [Stalin's] name in the sky" (Anderson, 2015, p. 113). Stalin's picture could be found "everywhere . . . with its kind smile and his hand raised in welcome" (Anderson, 2015, p. 113). At the same time, Anderson's narrative also underscores the individual and collective paranoia that also pervaded many citizens of the city.

How might a social studies teacher maximize the learning of *Symphony* by teaching about this cult of personality? An analysis of Stalinist propaganda posters (the Brown University [1940] library offers an introduction to Soviet propaganda posters and a gallery of images) is an excellent way to heighten student interest in this biography and the book's historical context—a repressive regime. According to John Medina (2014), "Vision is by far our most dominant sense, taking up half of our brain's resources" (p. 197). With this in mind, it is no wonder that many teachers and students find visual imagery so appealing. In fact, the analysis of images has gradually become a staple of social studies instruction, but it also has broad application to other content areas especially the English language arts.

The *Symphony* Cross-Disciplinary Activities

It is important to remember that Anderson's *Symphony* is being used to enhance student's understanding of the importance of Russia's role containing and stopping Germany's advance on the eastern front during World War II. The book highlights the suffering and efforts of the citizens of Leningrad and provides a rich description of the city during a specific span of time Several problems are uncovered: climate in several senses of the word—the actual challenges of weather, political climate, the city's sense of itself, and the social atmosphere; internal struggles within Russia while withstanding the German forces; the decay of social strata; and the consequences of a siege. Anderson captures the city's strength and determination by centering the story on the life and contributions of one of Leningrad's famous citizens,

Dmitri Shostakovich, and his seventh symphony—the Leningrad Symphony. It must be stated that a study of this account and its description of the artist, the citizens, and the city during World War II could be a complete college level course. Instead, we hint at the power of a series of pre-, during-, and post assignments that enhance the particular unit, but that could be gateway activities to student selected project-based learning activities that could lead to projects exploring biographies, memoirs, music (as a social source of propaganda, as the history of a specific piece and it performance and acceptance, the investigation of other music that has served as inspiration or protest in the time of war, warfare in World War II, the history of the siege in war, the conflict between the self-governance of a city or a state in the face of a stronger (or weaker) central government.

In the remainder of our chapter we use *Symphony* as the primary text, but actively describe several pre-, during-, and post activities that develop critical thinking skills thereby helping students develop a deeper understanding of the allied relationship between the Soviet Union (Russia) and the United States during World War II and demonstrate the Soviet's role in stopping the German advance on the Eastern Front. More specifically, the role of the citizens of Leningrad as they reacted to several "climates." How does the political climate, both within the country and in an international context, affect them? How do Leningraders confront and deal with both the emotional and physical climates exacerbated by a siege? How does Leningrad's social climate— especially as specifically represented by the music of Shostakovich and his fellow musicians—aid the city during this time of struggle. Answering these questions requires a blunt confrontation with the horrors of war, so teachers are encouraged to have a thoughtful preliminary conversation with their students before utilizing *Symphony* and the activities herein described. The following activities help guide students in ways that will help them read and grasp aspects of *Symphony* that illustrate the crucial contributions of this city.

BEFORE READING *SYMPHONY FOR THE CITY OF THE DEAD: DMITRI SHOSTAKOVICH AND THE SIEGE OF LENINGRAD*

Analyze Images

There are several instructional strategies for analyzing images. The Library of Congress' model offers a nonsequential process for image analysis summarized by three verbs: Observe ⇄ Reflect ⇄ Question. By contrast, the Visual Discovery strategy (VDS) from the Teacher's Curriculum Institute is a linear approach, which provides a focused and efficient method of analyzing images eventually leading students to the highest level of thinking—synthesis. For example, just as students begin reading *Symphony*, you might have students analyze a 1940 poster of the "Man of Steel" containing the slogan: "Under the banner of Lenin, with the leadership of Stalin, forward to the victory of Communism" found in Brown University's David Winton Bell Gallery. The heart of the five-step VDS involves a series of questions used to analyze images—in this case a poster—which spirals from gathering evidence to interpreting the evidence and, ultimately, making hypotheses (for a more detailed description of this strategy see Lobdell, Owens, & Bower, 2010, pp. 28–37). By incorporating an analysis of this poster (or any number of others) using the VDS, teachers can "spark student imagination" leading to heightened interest and understanding of *Symphony* (Anthony & Hopper, 2016, p. 32).

Step One

Use powerful images (with layers of meaning) such as the 1940 propaganda poster of Stalin to teach key concepts. In this poster, Stalin stands behind a podium with a statue of Vladimir Lenin and red banners in the background and a line of proletarian workers in the foreground with the caption: "Under the banner of Lenin, with the leadership of Stalin, forward to the victory of Communism."

Step Two

Project the selected image on a large screen arranging the desks in parliamentary seating, so students are facing each other (in order to facilitate discussion) with a wide aisle in the center leading to the image.

Step Three

Ask carefully sequenced and spiraling questions that lead to discovery:

Gathering Evidence. What do you see in this image? Identify key details from this poster (e.g., in the background a Statue of Lenin is gesturing forward, in the center Stalin is in a military uniform with a facial expression—both benign and wise—pointing in the same direction as his iconic predecessor, youthful workers in the foreground clutching the fruits of their labor, and the youth on the far right is grasping a book).

Interpreting the Evidence. What does the positioning of these individuals in the poster signify? What does the color red symbolize? When was this poster made? How does the slogan at the bottom of the poster and the book title (translated it says, *"Marx, Engels, Lenin, Stalin"*) complement one another. For each question, have students provide at least two pieces of evidence to support their interpretation.

Making Hypotheses. Why are the individuals featured in this poster gazing forward? Why was it important for this poster of Stalin to include symbolic references to Marx, Engels, and Lenin? Again, have students provide at least two pieces of evidence to support their hypothesis.

Step Four

Challenge students to read about the image and apply what they learn. In order to augment the information garnered from an analysis of the poster, students might read passages from informational texts including *Symphony* (pp. 103, 113).

Step Five

Have students interact with the images to demonstrate what they have learned. This final step of VDS challenges students to synthesize the information in the poster and textual source(s). One engaging way to do this is through an "Act-It-Out" activity. Ask student triads to step into the Stalin poster and carry on a symbolic conversation between Stalin, Lenin, and one of the workers or between three workers in the foreground. Encourage them to infuse their dialogue with information they have learned from analyzing the poster and reading the textual source(s). You may want to support this process with a script or role cards (including brief talking points) or, perhaps, have the students ad lib.

Survey

This could take the form of a traditional set of multiple choice or short answer questions or a digitized format where the teacher shows a series of images and allows time for the students identify them. The purpose of the survey can vary. It might be about the students' understanding of the relationship between the United States and Russia or it might be to see if they recognize or can respond to images of names from the period.

Music

Introduce classical music, introduce Shostakovich. Many students are not familiar with this musical genre. Class can begin with short clips of classical music that has been used in popular formats. For example, *The Lone Ranger* used a movement from Rossini's *William Tell Overture* and the movie, *V for Vendetta*, uses Tchaikovsky's *1812 Overture*. As students begin to see how older forms of music have been repurposed, it is easier to introduce them to more complex levels of classic music—including those that preceded Shostakovich and his contemporaries.

Biographical Introductions

This can be done in a variety of ways. Most teachers recognize that students understand books better if they have the necessary background knowledge that provides a foundation for further information. Teachers should gauge the knowledge base of their students and build on that information, accordingly.

WHILE READING *SYMPHONY FOR THE CITY OF THE DEAD: DMITRI SHOSTAKOVICH AND THE SIEGE OF LENINGRAD*

One of the prominent themes in this book is *siege*, which means: "a military operation in which enemy forces surround a [city] . . . , cutting off essential supplies, with the aim of compelling the surrender of those inside." Obviously, Leningrad was under siege by the fascist German army. But, in a larger sense, the Russian people were also under siege by their own government—an equally bloodthirsty and totalitarian regime, but communist. In this context, the arts and, more specifically, music was under siege especially those innovative composers, such as Shostakovich and, by association, his family, friends, and acquaintances. Anderson focuses on Shostakovich, in part, as a single example of how many scholars, artists, public employees, and others strove to maintain productivity, sanity, and family relationships under the strain of the Stalinist regime and the siege. The most difficult physical aspect of the siege's climate was the winter with its harsh weather and lack of food supplies. At the same time, it is clear in the text that the emotional and social climate was equally as challenging.

Primary Sources

By enhancing an event in the book through further research into primary sources, students can use their own smaller scale implementation of visual discovery, conduct a Google search for further explanations, or summarize the Quick Write or fifty-word summary. Teachers can also provide an explanation through a traditional lecture.

Quick Write

This activity can best be described as a journal writing activity, ranging from three to ten minutes. Their purpose is to conduct summary assessments that review what has been covered previously in class, what they have read, or what will be covered.

Fifty-Word Summary

Students pick three aspects of a theme and write concisely about it using exactly fifty words. They draft, edit, and rewrite in order to limit unnecessary adjectives and adverbs while focusing on essential information. A correct response covers the right information and has exactly fifty words.

Writing for Understanding

The sheer scope of suffering experienced by the residents during the second siege of Leningrad is chronicled in a *Symphony* chapter entitled, "The City of the Dead." The hardships were such that instead of using descriptive narrative, the survivors succinctly summarized their circumstances in stark terms, such as "*dirt, snowdrifts, snow, cold, darkness, starvation, death*" (p. 284). As the author observed, "It is as if there is no syntax, no grammar, that can contain their suffering" (p. 284). Likewise, students could read this chapter and assemble a comprehensive list of Leningrader privations—in essence a staccato of suffering—as a prewriting activity. These categories of suffering might include emotional, physical/medical, and weather-related hardships. As an ELA follow-up activity, each student would assume the role of a Leningrader who composes a series of journal entries about the tribulations of the siege (for a more detailed description of this strategy see Lobdell, Owens, & Bower, pp. 56–65).

AFTER READING *SYMPHONY FOR THE CITY OF THE DEAD: DMITRI SHOSTAKOVICH AND THE SIEGE OF LENINGRAD*

Timeline

Have student identify ten moments, including explanations and illustrations from primary sources. The top of their timeline would be dedicated to highlighting the major events in the history of Russia (Soviet Union), which occurred during the lifetime of Shostakovich, while the bottom of the timeline would focus on major events in the life of the composer himself.

Music

First, as a whole class, listen to a portion of Shostakovich *Symphony #7*—the Leningrad Symphony. At this point they should understand the extreme physical difficulties that the musicians faced. Many were near starvation and there was no escape from the cold; nevertheless, they summoned the energy to perform and the premiere was broadcast over radio. As individuals or in small groups, students can find images from the time period and create a visual accompaniment to a portion of the symphony. Next, students could develop a report on the history of *Symphony #7*, focusing on one of the following: how it was premiered in other countries during the war, how it has been received and reviewed over the last sixty years, and the reputation of a different part of Shostakovich's oeuvre (work).

Visual Representation of Casualties

Like soldiers on a far-flung battlefield who all claim to have been at the center of the engagement's bloodiest fighting, patriotic impulses can lead secondary students to narrowly attribute victory to the hardships experienced and contributions made by the United States; after all, we often say it is "The Greatest Generation." While there were, of course, great sacrifices made on the part of many Americans, *Symphony* opens a window to a less ethnocentric view of the suffering experienced by the major Allied powers. Ask students to glean the death toll figures in Leningrad in the aftermath of the 872-day siege, the longest in history (pp. 358–359, 362–363) (see table 5.1). Next, using these same pages, have students assemble the grim Soviet death toll and the destruction of infrastructure as a result of World War II:

Finally, invite students to create a pie chart or bar graph based on the military and civilian casualties suffered by the major Allied (France, Great Britain, United States, and Soviet Union) and Axis Powers (Germany, Italy, and Japan) using the statistics provided by the National World War II Museum website.

Table 5.1. The aftermath of the 872-day siege

Leningrad prewar population:	2.5 million
Leningrad postwar population:	575,000
Soviet war dead:	27 million
Soviet villages destroyed:	70,000
Soviet factories destroyed:	32,000
Soviet hospitals destroyed:	40,000
Soviet schools destroyed:	80,000
Soviet libraries destroyed:	43,000

EXTENSION ACTIVITIES BEYOND *SYMPHONY FOR THE CITY OF THE DEAD: DMITRI SHOSTAKOVICH AND THE SIEGE OF LENINGRAD*

Symphony provides an abundance of opportunities to make connections with the larger historical events, which serve as a backdrop for this biography. Strategic historical overviews are threaded throughout the book, which might be especially useful in the timeline activity, such as the events leading to the Russian Revolution (pp. 12–21) and Hitler's rise to power, the Molotov-Ribbentrop Pact, and the German invasion of the Soviet Union (pp. 151–170). Students can be invited to search for answers to these questions:

1. How is a siege defined, and how has it been used in the history of the world?
2. Would the current status of Aleppo, Syria, be considered a siege?
3. What was the relationship between Russia and the United States during World War II?
4. How might the term *climate* in a social studies context be related to setting and tone in a literature context.

CONCLUSION

In a collaborative effort, both teachers need to share their subject area expertise. Such expertise includes more than their context knowledge. It also includes how well they have mastered teaching strategies that thoughtfully engage students from the beginning of the unit through to the end. For example, if understanding various definitions of climate throughout the unit becomes an essential question for both teachers, students begin more complex analysis. Defining the political culture—and climate—represented by a visual discovery activity in a social studies class focuses the students' attention on the political climate of Leningrad and the Soviet Union even as they track the toll of the German siege. Later, the English teacher can build on and/or assess how students understand and articulate the political climate displayed in a middle chapter of the book through the use of a quick write or fifty-word summary. Thus, ironically, the teachers are also simultaneously building a climate that creates a collaborative sense between the two subjects. Hopefully, students will be inclined to study and value a thoughtful social studies curriculum. At the same time, both English and social studies teachers supplement the study of historical period and specific events with the inclusion of YA nonfiction texts.

Annotated List of Related YA Literature

The Family Romanov: Murder, Rebellion & the Fall of Imperial Russia by Candace Fleming (304 pp.)

Told in three stories, this novel offers readers a window into the Romanovs themselves, the revolution that began with the workers' strikes of 1905 to Lenin's rise to power in 1917, and the personal stories of the peasants, the men and women who struggled to survive in Russia.

The Nazi Hunters: How a Team of Spies and Survivors Captured the World's Most Notorious Nazi by Neal Boscomb (256 pp.)

Fifteen years after the end of World War II, a group of Jewish men come together to capture and bring to justice Nazi war criminal, Adolf Eichmann.

Imprisoned: The Betrayal of Japanese Americans during World War II by Martin W. Sandler (176 pp.)

After the bombing of Pearl Harbor, hysteria broke out sending over 120,000 Japanese Americans into internment camps. With no notice they were forced to leave homes, businesses and possessions to move into these camps for the duration of World War II. Their story is told in this book through photographs, interviews, quotes, and sidebars (backed up with extensive research).

Bomb: The Race to Build—and Steal—the World's Most Dangerous Weapon by Steve Sheinkin (272)

This nonfiction YA book is the story of the plotting, risk-taking, deceit, and genius that created the world's most formidable weapon—the atomic bomb.

REFERENCES

Anderson, M. T. (2015). *Symphony for the city of the dead: Dmitri Shostakovich and the siege of Leningrad*. Somerville, MA: Candlewick Press.

Anthony, K., & Hopper, P. (2016). Fostering inquiry through pairing children's literature with historical photographs. *Oregon Journal for the Social Studies, 4*(2), 31–40.

Boscomb, N. (2013). *The Nazi hunters: How a team of spies and survivors captured the world's most notorious Nazi*. New York: Arthur A. Levine Books.

Brown University (1940). Poster of the Man of Steel. David Winton Bell Gallery. Retrieved from http://library.brown.edu/cds/Views_and_Reviews/item_views/medium_itemlevel_posters.php?id=154&view_type=medium_index.

Ellis, E. G., and Esler, A. (2005). *World history: Connections to today*. Upper Saddle River, NJ: Prentice Hall.

Fleming, C. (2014). *The family Romanov: Murder, rebellion & the fall of imperial Russia.* New York: Schwartz & Wade.

Hesse, K. (1997). *Out of the dust.* New York: Scholastic Press.

Knowles, J. (2000). *A separate peace.* Austin, TX: Holt, Rinehart and Winston.

Lee, H. (1960). *To kill a mockingbird.* London, UK: Heinemann.

Lobdell, J., Owens, S., & Bower, B. (2010). *Bringing learning alive!* Rancho Cordova, CA: Teachers' Curriculum Institute.

Medina, J. (2014). *Brain rules.* Seattle, WA: Pear Press.

National World War II Museum. Military and civilian casualties suffered in WWII. Retrieved from http://www.nationalww2museum.org/learn/education/for-students/ww2history/ww2-by-the-numbers/world-wide-deaths.html.

Sandler, M. W. (2013). *Imprisoned: The betrayal of Japanese Americans during World War II.* New York: Bloomsbury.

Saxe, J. G. (2005). *The blind men and the elephant.* Saxe JG (December 2005). Wikipedia, the free encyclopedia.

Sheinkin, S. (2012). *Bomb: The race to build—and steal—the world's most dangerous weapon.* New York: Flash Point.

Tuchman, B. W. (1981). *Practicing history: Selected essays.* New York: Ballantine Books.

Chapter 6

Number the Stars: World War II and Young Adult Literature

Jason L. O'Brien and Brooke Eisenbach

World War II is the largest global conflict in the history of the world, both in regard to the deaths it caused (estimated 50 and 80 million) and for its whole-sale destruction worldwide. Its conclusion left the United States as a global superpower, while much of Europe's infrastructure was destroyed. As such, this conflict constitutes an important part of the social studies curriculum for both middle and high school students. It is nearly impossible to understand geopolitics of the second half of the twentieth century without knowing the events which transpired during the war. Of particular importance, is for students to learn about one of the worst examples of genocide in human history. Specifically, the mass murder of Jews, persons with disabilities, the elderly, gypsies, and those identified as homosexuals under Hitler's Third Reich. Students should be familiar with these events so that they can fully comprehend the capacity for human cruelty as well as to act to prevent such occurrences in the future.

Other than the teacher, students' main resource for learning about these events is often their textbook. While textbooks have their uses as a resource, researchers have criticized textbooks for being used as "ideological weapons" (White, 2008, p. 1), for containing gender bias (Ndura, 2004), for containing factual errors (Loewen, 1995), and for being inaccessible and boring due to their reliance on academic prose and vocabulary (Pingel, 1999). One way to increase student understanding of historical events is to include readings which are of high interest to the students, thus adding increased motivation to learn (Hidi, 2001). This chapter will provide activities and strategies to incorporate the book *Number the Stars* (1989) by Lois Lowry in the social studies classroom. This young adult (YA) book offers students a fictionalized but his-torically accurate account of the tribulations experienced by one Jewish family living in Denmark during the German occupation of their country. Through

55

the inclusion of this book, students are provided narratives which describe the realities of the Holocaust as told through the eyes of adolescents who lived it. By including such literature, hopefully students will experience an affective connection to the characters, many of whom are their own age. As an added benefit, middle and high school students can learn about topics which are routinely overlooked in traditional coverage of World War II and the Holocaust (e.g., impacts of Nazi occupation in "satellite" countries, experiences of children during the war, and instances of bravery by "ordinary" citizens). These stories have the potential to teach students about courage and virtuous behavior, should they ever be placed in a situation which requires either.

In this chapter, the authors will provide teachers with a framework for studying the Holocaust through *Number the Stars* (Lowry, 1989), specifically exploring the theme of courage. Courage demonstrated by adolescents who experienced the Holocaust offers an access point for students to begin to examine their own opportunities to act as agents of justice in the face of tyranny and oppression.

SUMMARY OF *NUMBER THE STARS* BY LOIS LOWRY (156 PP.)

Number the Stars is a fictional story which begins in Denmark in 1943 during the time the country was occupied by Germany. The main character, Annmarie Johansen, lives with her sister and parents in Copenhagen under the watchful eyes of German soldiers. Annmarie's best friend is named Ellen Rosen, a Jew. One evening at the beginning of the Jewish New Year, Ellen is brought to live with Annmarie as her sister, to escape mass deportations enacted by German soldiers on the Jews of Denmark. When some of these troops enter his home searching for Ellen's parents, Annmarie's father convinces the soldiers that despite her dark hair, Ellen is his daughter. Without telling them why, Mrs. Johansen takes her daughters and Ellen to visit their uncle Henrik, a fisherman who lives on the coast. Unbeknownst to the reader, Henrik is also secretly a member of the Danish Resistance helping Jews escape across the North Sea to safety in Sweden.

After Annmarie's family arrives at Henrik's, Ellen's parents join the group and a plan is made to smuggle the family aboard Henrik's boat to safety the following morning. Ellen's mother leads Ellen and her parents to Henrik's boat, but the group is supposed to bring a special package which gets inadvertently dropped by one of the escapees. Annmarie finds the package on the ground upon her mother's return from delivering the Rosens and realizes that she must run through the woods at night to deliver it to Henrik if the trip is to be successful. After a tense encounter with soldiers in which Annmarie displays admirable courage, she delivers the package and the Rosens are able to escape to Sweden and safety.

While a work of fiction, the story is based on actual events which happened during World War II as many Danes placed themselves at great risk and sometimes sacrificed their lives to save the lives of others. Due to the courageous efforts of ordinary Danes, more than 99 percent of the nation's 7,800 Jews were able to escape by sea to Sweden. The story is a testament to courage and sacrifice and the afterword contains a powerful statement quoted from a twenty-one-year-old Danish freedom fighter who penned it the night before he was put to death: "and I want you all to remember—that you must not dream yourselves back to the times before the war, but the dream for you all, young and old, must be to *create an ideal of human decency, and not a narrow-minded and prejudiced one*" (emphasis ours) (p. 137).

BEFORE READING *NUMBER THE STARS*

Provide Background Information

Denmark's Role in World War II

Since most middle and high school students have very little background information on Denmark's role in World War II, teachers should first display a map of Europe so that students are aware of Denmark's location, both in relation to Germany and to its neutral neighbor Sweden. By showing a comparison of military resources between Germany and Denmark (i.e., number of troops, number of tanks, size of navy), students will understand why Denmark surrendered to Germany instead of having its soldiers slaughtered by *Blitzkrieg* tactics utilized by German generals. After examining the differences in the two countries' military resources, students can be asked to complete a "cost-benefit" organizer on the topic of "Fighting the German Army." Specifically, students should be able to list both the benefits and costs of resisting German occupation through military efforts. Hopefully, students will understand that when faced with overwhelming military superiority, the most prudent action oftentimes is to surrender to "fight another day."

Danish Navy

The book mentions the scuttling of the Danish navy by King Christian X to avoid having its ships commandeered by the German navy. The Danish Naval History website contains primary documents such as newspaper articles and photographs of the entire fleet as it lay partially submerged in the port waters at the Royal Dockyard in Copenhagen. The destruction of the fleet offers historical context of the events which occurred just before the book begins.

Final Solution

Teachers should also make sure that students are aware of the policies enacted by Adolf Hitler and Nazi Germany under the auspices of his "Final Solution." Specifically, students should know that by this time, most Jews were forced to relocate to labor camps or concentration camps, which had the ultimate purpose of starving or working them to death. Showing pictures of the treatment of Jews in these camps can add an affective component to the learning, which researchers have found can significantly increase retention and recall of such events (Jensen, 2008). A PBS website contains historical photographs and a timeline of the orders issued by the German government which mandated the forced migration of Jews to ghettos and later to concentration camps. This site also contains a guide for educators and discussion questions for use after students have learned sufficient background on the topic.

A Classroom Museum

One effective strategy when studying a time period in modern history is for students to create a "classroom museum." For this topic, the internet contains a plethora of resources which students can print and bring to class to add to their understanding of the time period. Each student can be asked to find and bring to class three pictures depicting this episode in history. Have students form teams of three or four through the creation of logical groupings based on the pictures. Have each team arrange the pictures for display on poster board or on the walls of the classroom. Have students research, write, and then record information about their pictures on their phones or other recording device. By attaching headphones, visitors and other students can listen to the recorded information while looking at the photos, giving the feel of being in a museum while at school.

Social and Emotional Preparation

The Holocaust was an event encompassing unimaginable horror and devastation. As students today are far removed from this historic moment in time, it is imperative teachers prepare to address the social and emotional needs of students as they engage in the study of the Holocaust. Teachers want to avoid engaging students in a superficial understanding of the atrocities of this time, while also avoiding oversimplification of the emotions running rampant within the hearts and minds of the people. As students prepare to read *Number the Stars*, they can initiate a personal reader memo journal. Throughout the unit of study, students will utilize their personal journal to memo their ideas, feelings, questions, and connections to the text and the information they learn regarding the people and events surrounding this moment in history. In memoing their experience, they can self-reflect on the thoughts and feelings that surface as a result of engaging in a study of such a monumental moment in history.

WHILE READING *NUMBER THE STARS*

Inspire Courage and Empathy

Tell the students that an important theme in the book is that of courage. Ask the students to find passages in which the main character, Annmarie, exhibited bravery. Once identified, have the students copy the passage verbatim, including all bibliographic information. In groups of three or four, ask students to share their passage and explain why they thought Annmarie's actions were courageous. As an empathy exercise, ask the students to write a journal entry as if they were Annmarie asking them how they would have responded in the same situation. By doing this, historical content becomes relevant to students' lives and requires them to make a decision whether to act or whether to acquiesce to the German authorities.

Unpacking Upstander Actions

Adolescents are often faced with moments in which they must decide if they will be bystanders or upstanders. Will they take a stand for a peer who is the victim of bullying? Will they set aside their own fear of retaliation and dare to take action for the betterment of others? *Number the Stars* invites student connection and conversation regarding the place of upstander actions in the face of adversity. Throughout the novel, Annmarie and her family act as upstanders, finding ways to help neighbors and Jewish families. As an upstander exercise, students can begin by journaling moments when they faced a choice—to act as a bystander, collaborator, perpetrator, or upstander. From here, students can examine current events that also depict everyday citizens who have taken action to help someone in need. Drawing upon these connections, students can unpack moments in the text when characters choose to remain a bystander, or act as an upstander. They can engage in a classroom debate or conversation regarding the realities of taking action to help someone when faced with potential risk to one's self or one's family. The goal of this conversation is greater understanding of the complexities involved in such a choice, and furthering student empathy for those who were faced with such a decision in a time of unspeakable fear.

Guided Imagery Exercise

Much like historical role plays and simulations, guided imagery can be an effective tool to help students connect to and understand content more effectively than traditional teacher-lead instruction (Beck & Kosnik, 2006). In a guided imagery, the teacher presents a realistic scenario which requires students to imagine themselves as participants in a particular historical situation. After the teacher describes a scenario for students, they are then required to write a response indicating their thoughts, feelings, or actions. In the story *Number the Stars*, the protagonist and supporting characters are faced with difficult decisions which require bravery and conviction. Having students engage in this activity can allow them the opportunity to vicariously experience these events in a safe environment as well as give them practice in the decision-making process, an important part of informed and effective citizenship.

To begin this activity, the teacher should tell the students, "Today we are going to take an imaginary trip into the year 1943. Assume a comfortable position in your chair and close your eyes. Try to clear your mind and relax." After the students have done so, the teacher should continue by saying:

Today is September 30, 1943, but you are the same age you are today. You live in Copenhagen, Denmark, with your parents and your younger sister. For three years, Germany has occupied your country and every day, as you walk to and from school, you must pass under the watchful eyes of frightening German soldiers with their polished boots and rifles. Recently, all the Jewish shops have been ordered to close and your parents told you that all the Jews have been arrested and sent to work camps by the Germans. You overheard your parents talking at dinner about an article they read in an illegal newspaper that said that women and children who were too young or too weak to work were killed in gas chambers and then buried in mass graves.

These stories worry you because your best friend Ellen Rosen is Jewish, and you have not seen her since she and her parents fled to escape being arrested. You miss spending time with her after school because she is your best friend.

Just after dark, while you are reading a book in your room, you hear men shouting in German and then you hear gunshots CRACK! CRACK! Seconds later, there is a knock at your bedroom window. You walk over and pull back your curtains and you see Ellen Rosen covered in dirt and looking terrified. You quickly open the window and Ellen climbs into your room. She drops to the floor and says "Quick! Hide me. I escaped from the train and the Germans know I'm in this area. Please help me!"

You have a choice to make. If you allow Ellen to stay in your home, you risk having the German soldiers find her and you are sure they will punish your family and you. If you notify the authorities, Ellen will surely be shot or sent to a concentration camp where she will undoubtedly die.

After a conspicuous pause, have the students open their eyes and continue

Please take out a sheet of paper and a writing utensil. At the top of your paper write "Daily Journal Entry for September 30, 1943" and write "Today, Ellen Rosen came to me and asked me to hide her." Put yourself in the same position that Annmarie and her parents were in during the story. You will have ten minutes to write a journal entry describing what course of action you chose regarding Ellen and why you chose to do so.

After students have completed their journals, ask several to share their ideas with the class. If students are reticent to share, the teacher can offer to collect all the stories and read several chosen randomly so that students do not know who authored the journal. As a debriefing activity, the teacher can ask the following questions to encourage discussion:

• What was the most important factor which influenced your decision to hide or not hide Ellen? Why?
• Many people chose not to break laws to help Jews escape or to hide. How should history judge these people?
• Were the Danes and other people who broke laws to help Jews being "good citizens" of their respective countries?
• Under what circumstances would you break the law today to help someone else?
• Are there any laws we have today in our country that you feel are unfair or discriminatory toward one group of people?
• (optional) What is the bravest thing you've ever done in your life that put you in danger?

AFTER READING *NUMBER THE STARS*

The ultimate goal of teaching social studies is to provide students "the content knowledge, intellectual skills, and civic values necessary for fulfilling the duties of citizenship" (National Council for the Social Studies, 2005, p. 1). The central theme in *Number the Stars* is that of courage and standing up to injustice. After reading the book, the teacher can share with students the three different types of citizens—the Personally-Responsible Citizen, the Participatory Citizen, and the Justice Oriented Citizen—as identified by Westheimer and Kahne (2004). Specifically, these researchers identified a "social justice orientation" held by individuals regarding citizenship, which has as its goal to help students understand not only how to identify problems with society, but as importantly, to help students understand that they can and should play an active role to ameliorate these problems.

After sharing this citizenship orientation, the teacher can provide the prompt "Was Annemarie a good citizen? Why or why not?" Students should be able to identify that even though Annmarie and her family broke laws imposed by Germans, their actions were nevertheless morally correct. These discussions regarding the responsibilities of citizenship can lead to a more-developed conceptualization of the topic which hopefully includes some aspect of social justice. Armed with this knowledge, students can then begin to identify other historic and contemporary examples of people who violated laws which were unjust but who were ultimately vindicated for their virtuous actions.

Finally, we have provided fourteen additional YA books that can be read about children facing difficult situations during World War II. In partners or in threes, students can choose one of the books to read and pose their own questions to the class, discussing the responsibilities of citizenship displayed in their respective texts.

EXTENSION ACTIVITIES BEYOND *NUMBER THE STARS*

A Timeline

As a review of *Number the Stars* as well as the entire unit, create a timeline of the events that happened in the novel as well as in history. Take butcher paper or large display sheets and tape them to the wall of the classroom. This paper should be long enough to allow ample room for students to write information and vignettes contained in the book. Segment the paper by year starting with 1939 and ending with 1945, to demonstrate the years in which World War II occurred. Be sure that the timeline is titled and drawn accurately to scale. Draw a horizontal line about one third of the way down the entire length of the paper. While students are reading other books related to World War II, have them paraphrase and jot down on the scrap paper dates and information contained in their reading material. On the top third of the butcher paper, have students record historic dates with their corresponding events in black ink. On the bottom two thirds, have students write the corresponding vignettes about the people they are reading about. It is helpful to keep the vignettes color-coded by books. By having students include their initials, those who want to discuss a specific occurrence can consult "the author," who in this case becomes "the expert." As information accumulates on the timeline, students get to see their contributions to the project and can gain an understanding of the chronology of events of the war.

Examples of Prejudice Today

Each student is to find a newspaper or magazine account of some act of discrimination today. Students are often shocked by the many forms of prejudice and become painfully aware of the relevancy of World War II to us today, especially when they read about genocide in Darfur and ethnic cleansing in the former Yugoslavia between 1992 and 1995. Currently, there are several hundred "hate groups" operating in the United States as identified by the Southern Poverty Law Center. Even in 2017, there has been an increase in arson and vandalizing of Muslim and Jewish community centers and churches. By having students research current examples of such discrimination and violence, students can begin to see that certain minority groups still face discrimination and violence in our own society. From here, students should engage in critical discussion and action in an attempt to instill hope and justice for those directly affected by such discrimination.

CONCLUSION

World War II provides many lessons to students of history. Hopefully by studying it, students are reminded of the capacity of human beings to perpetuate cruel acts on other groups, most often under the auspices of "nationalism" or some other politically motivated ideology, while also bearing witness to the power of the individual to take action for the betterment of others. Having students read *Number the Stars* (and other YA literature on the topic) is one way to increase interest and engagement with the topic of the Holocaust, while at the same time allowing students to learn of the often untold stories of everyday citizens who were caught in the conflagration. Ultimately, teachers should want their students to learn from these historical atrocities, because if we do not learn history's mistakes, we are doomed as a society to repeat them.

Annotated List of Other Related YA Novels

Anne Frank and Me by Cherie Bennett and Jeff Gottesfeld (287 pp.)

This easy-to-read adaptation of the 1998 play by the same title tells the story of Nicole Burns, a tenth-grade student who questions the purpose of reading *The Diary of Anne Frank*. Nicole suddenly finds herself transported back to Nazi-occupied France. Here, she meets Anne Frank and learns first hand the true value of studying the Holocaust.

London Calling by Edward Bloor (304 pp.)

Martin Conway, like many seventh graders, hates school and finds himself unsure of his place in the world. When his grandmother dies, she leaves him a vintage World War II radio. Through the radio, he teleports back to 1940s

London and meets Jimmy, a teen who pleas for Martin's help. Through a series of alternating story lines, Martin seeks to expose the truths of his ancestors and provide help to a teen in need.

We Are Witnesses: Five Diaries of Teenagers Who Died in the Holocaust by Jacob Boas (208 pp.)

Boas, born in the Westerbork Concentration Camp in Holland, weaves commentary and narrative in sharing the stories of five teenagers who journaled their personal experiences during the Holocaust. In sharing the voices of David Rubinowicz, Yitzhak Rudashevski, Moshe Flinker, Eva Heyman, and Anne Frank, Boas bears witness to the experiences of the youth and families who lived and died as a result of persecution.

Memories of My Life in a Polish Village: 1930–1949 by Toby Knobel Fluek (110 pp.)

Toby Fluek was a small Jewish girl growing up in Czernica, Poland, at the onset of World War II. By the war's end, only she and her mother had survived the atrocities that devastated her home and family. Now an artist living in New York City, Fluek shares her story through her paintings and prose.

I Am David by Anne Holm (256 pp.)

Twelve-year-old David has lived his entire life behind the walls of a concentration camp in Eastern Europe. He knows nothing of life or freedom outside the camp; but, when he is presented with the opportunity to escape, David seizes it and begins his journey to Denmark in search of hope in a strange, new world.

Room in the Heart by Sonia Levitin (285 pp.)

Told primarily from the alternating perspectives of two young Danes, this novel chronicles the events of Germany's invasion of Denmark as experienced by those directly affected. After learning of the Germans' plans to capture all of the Jewish people in Denmark, Julie rushes her family to Sweden by boat. Her friend and co-narrator, Niels, joins the resistance while his friend, Emil, is captivated by the power of the Germans. This powerful narrative shares the story of how the Danes fought the Nazi occupation and managed to save almost all of Denmark's Jews.

Tug of War by Joan Lingard (208 pp.)

As their family flees the Russian invasion of Latvia in 1944, Hugo and Astra, fourteen-year-old Latvian twins, are separated by chaos and a crowd of refugees. Astra and her family are forced to move from camp to camp, facing adversity and unspeakable challenge. Meanwhile, Hugo ends up in Hamburg, Germany, where a family takes care of him until the end of the war. Despite the adversity, Hugo and Astra persevere in their belief that they will one day be reunited.

No Pretty Pictures: A Child of War by Anita Lobel (193 pp.)

At the age of five, Anita Lobel is forced to flee her home in Krakow, Poland as Nazi forces invade her hometown. Her parents send her, and her brother, to live with their Catholic nanny in the countryside. Eventually, the two are discovered and deported to a concentration camp where they live until the liberation. In this powerful memoir, Lobel shares her unfettered experiences in Nazi-occupied Europe as told through the eyes of a child.

In My Enemy's House by Carol Matas (167 pp.)

Marisa was fortunate to inherit her father's blonde hair and blue eyes. After she loses her family at the hand of the Nazis, she takes on the identity of a young Polish girl and goes to work as a servant for a Nazi family in Germany. As she spends more time and grows closer with the family, she finds herself coming to terms with some tough questions about her basic beliefs of humanity.

Four Perfect Pebbles by Lila Perl and B. Lazan (130 pp.)

Five-year-old Marion Blumenthal Lazan and her family fled Germany and traveled to Holland in an attempt to escape the Nazis. Unfortunately, their ship to America was fatally delayed and the Germans invaded Holland. The Blumenthals were deported to Bergen Belsen, where Marion, clinging to the hope that her family would one day be freed together, collects four pebbles from the camp to symbolize the members of her family. This riveting memoir shares a story of determination and survival under the most dire of circumstances.

We Were Not Like Other People by Ephraim Sevela (216 pp.)

This novel, based on the author's own lived experiences, tells the story of a Russian Jewish teenager who is separated from his parents at the onset of World War II. A Russian peasant woman and her daughters find him exhausted and nearly starved. They nurse him back to health, allowing him to eventually return home and be reunited with his family. His life is a test of survival and perseverance.

Milkweed by Jerry Spinelli (208pp.)

As a young boy, Misha Pilsudski has had several names—Stopthief, Stupid, Jew, and Gypsy. He experiences life in technicolor and dreams in poetic observation of the world. When the "Jackboots" or Nazis march into town, he imagines life as a part of this powerful parade. Uri, another homeless boy surviving in the street of Warsaw during World War II, is older and more aware of the realities that surround them. Misha learns from Uri that the Nazis are not ones to emulate but to outsmart.

Behind the Secret Window: A Memoir of a Hidden Childhood during World War Two by Nelly S. Toll (161 pp.)

The author was only six years old when the Nazis invaded Poland. With the help of some Gentiles, Nelly and her mother go into hiding. She is given watercolors and paper to help her pass the time. For the two years they are in hiding, Nelly journals her fears, hopes, and dreams through her words and artwork.

The Book Thief by Markus Zusak (560 pp.)

Death narrates through the use of poetic syntax the story of Liesel Meminger, a young orphan growing up in a small town outside of Munich, Germany, in the early 1940s. The Nazis are in power, rounding up Jews and forcing German children to participate in the Hitler Youth. Liesel soon learns that her foster parents are hiding a Jew from the Nazis. Throughout the story, Liesel steals books because reading is what helps her survive; and, in the end, it is her story that Death finds to be captivating.

REFERENCES

Beck, C., & Kosnik, C. (2006). *Innovations in teacher education: A social constructivist approach*. New York: State University of New York Press.

Bennett, C., & Gottesfeld, J. (2001). *Anne Frank and me*. New York: Puffin Books.

Bloor, E. (2006). *London calling*. New York: Knopf Books for Young Readers.

Boas, J. (2009). *We are witnesses: Five diaries of teenagers who died in the Holocaust*. New York: Square Fish.

Danish Naval History. *August 29, 1943—the turning point*. Retrieved from http://www.navalhistory.dk/English/History/1939_1945/us_safari.htm.

Fluek, T. (1990). Memories of my life in a Polish village, 1930–1949. New York: Knopf.

Holm, A. (1963). *I am David*. Boston, MA: HMH Books for Young Readers.

Jensen, E. (2008). *Brain-based learning: The new paradigm of teaching* (2nd ed.). Thousand Oaks, CA: Corwin Press.

Levitin, S. (2003). *Room in the heart*. New York: Dutton Juvenile.

Lingard, J. (1992). *Tug of war*. New York: Puffin Books.

Lobel, A. (2008). *No pretty pictures: A child of war*. New York: HarperCollins Books.

Loewen, J. (1995). *Lies my teacher told me: Everything your American history textbook got wrong*. New York: Simon & Schuster.

Lowry, L. (1989). *Number the stars*. Boston, MA: Houghton Mifflin.

Lowry, L. (2011, 1989). *Number the stars*. New York: Houghton Mifflin Harcourt.

Matas, C. (2000). *In my enemy's house*. New York: Simon Pulse.

National Council for the Social Studies (2005). *Mission statement*. Retrieved from http://www.socialstudies.org/about.

Ndura, E. (2004). ESL and cultural bias: An analysis of elementary through high school textbooks in the western United States of America. *Language, Culture & Curriculum, 17*(2), 143–153.

Perl, L., & Lazan, B. (1996). *Four perfect pebbles: A Holocaust story*. New York: Greenwillow Books.

Pingel, F. (1999). *UNESCO guidebook on textbook research and textbook revision*. Hannover, Germany: Verlag Hahnsche Buchhandlung.

Sevela, E. (1989). *We were not like other people*. New York: Harper and Row.

Southern Poverty Law Center. Hate map. Retrieved from https://www.splcenter.org/hate-map.

Spinelli, J. (2003). *Milkweed*. New York: Scholastic.

Toll, N. S. (2003). *Behind the secret window: A memoir of a hidden childhood during World War Two*. New York: Puffin Books.

Westheimer, J., & Kahne, J. (2004). What kind of citizen? The politics of education for democracy. *American Educational Research Journal, 41*(2), 237–269.

White, H. (2008). The historical event. *A Journal of Feminist Culture, 19*(2), 9–34.

Zusak, M. (2005). *The book thief*. New York: Knopf Books for Young Readers.

Chapter 7

Using the Peritextual Literacy Framework with Young Adult Biographies: Introducing Peritextual Functions with Adolescents in Social Studies

Shelbie Witte, Melissa Gross, and Don Latham

Young adult (YA) biographies play an integral role in the lives of adolescents by highlighting key moments in history through engaging lenses and offering adolescents the opportunity to know innumerable people; and in the process, deepening their understanding of themselves and the intricacies of society (Carlson, 1980). We know from the research that YA literature can motivate adolescents to read (Blasingame, 2007; Groenke & Scherff, 2010, Lesesne, 2003; Miller, 2013), with motivation being a pillar to developing lifelong readers and success in academic and disciplinary literacy (Guthrie & Coddington, 2009; Waters & Jenkins, 2015).

As teachers and librarians, we have also seen the rapid expansion of the YA nonfiction genre, targeting adolescents who are voracious readers of nonfiction topics but who are unlikely to be motivated by or engaged with fiction or YA fiction. Young adult nonfiction, such as biographies, strengthens students' twenty-first-century skills such as information, global, economic, and critical literacy (Marinak & Gambrell, 2009; Partnership for 21st Century Skills, 2009).

By using YA nonfiction in the disciplines, teachers can guide students to think critically about YA nonfiction texts, and scaffold their learning to build their background knowledge on historical people and events while developing critical thinking about historical and contemporary issues in society (Alsup, 2013; Hayes & Tierney, 1982; Lafferty, 2014; Sheffield, Chisholm, and Howell, 2015). The complexities of nonfiction content and text structures, coupled with the complexities of the discipline, often cause confusion for content area teachers not trained in reading instruction (Dobbs, Ippolito, & Charner-Laird, 2016; Vacca & Vacca, 1999; Young, Moss, &

Cornwell, 2007). Content area teachers, eager to learn successful pedagogical approaches, will find the Peritextual Literacy Framework (PLF) is one such approach that provides a scaffold to assist readers in understanding content and thinking critically about a text.

Through a teacher and librarian collaborative approach, we discuss methods of using YA biography along with the PLF in middle school social studies. We use Phillip Hoose's *Claudette Colvin: Twice toward Justice* as a working example.

CLAUDETTE COLVIN: TWICE TOWARD JUSTICE BY PHILLIP HOOSE (160 PP.)

In March of 1955, African American teenager Claudette Colvin was arrested in Montgomery, Alabama, after refusing to relinquish her bus seat to a white passenger. Colvin's act of civil disobedience occurred nine months before Rosa Parks, an adult, refused to give up her bus seat; yet, Parks' action was widely celebrated, both at the time and in the years since, while Colvin's name fell into obscurity.

The book seeks to reclaim an important part of Civil Rights history in the United States by demonstrating the important role Colvin played in helping to raise awareness and galvanize the African American community. It also sheds light on why Colvin was seen by Civil Rights leaders as not being an appropriate "face" for the Movement; whereas, they found Parks much more acceptable. The two justices referred to in the subtitle are first, the eventual end of segregated buses in Montgomery and throughout the South; and second, the long-delayed recognition of Claudette Colvin's contribution to the Civil Rights Movement.

The book is amply illustrated with photographs from the time period and also contains material from interviews the author conducted with the adult Claudette Colvin. It represents a particularly effective way to introduce the Civil Rights Movement to middle-grade students by showing that a teenager just like them was able to help effect social change, although not without significant personal cost. While the book is available in both hardback and paperback format, we use the paperback version, as it is the more economical choice for classroom use.

BEFORE READING *CLAUDETTE COLVIN: TWICE TOWARD JUSTICE*

The Peritextual Literacy Framework

The Peritextual Literacy Framework (PLF), developed by Gross and Latham (ALAN Grant, 2016), is an extension of the paratext theory developed by

Genette (1997). Paratext refers to various things that surround or point to the main text in a work. There are two types of paratext: peritext and epitext. Peritext refers to things that surround the text, such as a table of contents, endorsements, a glossary, or index. Epitext refers to things that are not part of the work as it is presented but which point to the work such as book reviews, author correspondence, and the publisher's web page.

The PLF extends Genette's theory by explicating the functions of peritext in relation to a work. The PLF organizes these functions into six categories: production, promotional, intratextual, navigational, supplemental, and documentary (each is described in detail below). These functions can be used to categorize the various peritextual elements discussed by Genette and other writers in discussing media. The number and types of peritextual elements that are contained in a work vary, which is to say that various media will incorporate different types of peritext into the presentation of a work. For example, not every book has a table of contents or an index.

Whatever peritextual elements are part of the presentation of the text, they allow readers—if they pay attention to them—to assess the text by determining how it is organized, what the author is trying to achieve, how easy or difficult it is to navigate, and to gain a sense about the credibility of the text. Readers can also use peritext to determine their motivation to engage with a text and to construct a mental model that will help them approach the text if they choose to engage with it. Most of the functions of the PLF can be used flexibly in the pre-, during-, and post-reading stages. As a working example, we offer the following approaches based specifically on *Claudette Colvin.*

Traditionally, critical pre-reading activities have been designed to guide students to make predictions about text; give their personal, text-to-self connections to the topic of the text; and give their personal opinions of the topic. By focusing on the peritextual functions within the pre-reading phase, students are drawn to the elements within the nonfiction text that schematically prepare them to move to the during-reading phase. These functions guide them to ask questions, the key to student learning. These functions also move students to apply disciplinary tools to think critically, draw conclusions, and make informed decisions based on their conclusions.

Promotional

Promotional elements provide a kind of interface between the work and potential readers, working to make the case that the work is worth the reader's time. Typical examples of promotional elements are blurbs that endorse the work, author biographies, and lists of other works by the author. Examining how these elements work can provide an opportunity to discuss the use of claims in writing related to introducing a claim about a topic or issue, distinguishing between claim and evidence, and logically organizing evidence.

These elements are supported by the "Key Ideas and Details" standard of the Standards for History/Social Studies, which ask students to cite specific textual evidence to support analysis of primary and secondary sources.

Claudette Colvin demonstrates a number of these elements including the presence of award medals on the cover and promotional statements such as, "The acclaimed true story of the girl who changed history" and "With a new afterword by the author." The back cover sports a summary of the work and endorses the credibility of the content with statements such as, "Based on extensive interviews," "National Book Award-winning work," and "First in-depth account." The back cover also lists major awards the book has received, quotes from review outlets, and includes even a quote from Claudette Colvin herself. On the free endpaper, a full list of the awards bestowed on this work are presented, followed by two full pages of excerpts from reviews and then by a list of other titles by the author. The last page of the book presents the author's biography.

Promotional elements are important to consider in the pre-reading stage if they are they present. Teachers and librarians can point out that these elements represent "selling points." They can help students as potential consumers of the work to think about these elements and to what extent they affect students' views of the work: Is it credible? Is it important or not? Students can also consider how well the promotional elements are doing their job. Does considering these elements affect their desire to engage with the work? What kind of expectations do students have, given the promotional information? Is reading this book going to be interesting, fun, or hard work? Promotional elements can also be considered after the book is read to see how the reading experience held up to the promises the promotional elements made about the work.

Production

The production function within the PLF is comprised of elements that provide information about who is responsible for a work such as the author and publisher. Production elements are typically used to uniquely identify a work, enabling readers to locate a particular work and to know what work he or she has in hand. Production elements can also play a role in helping readers assess a work. For example, the date of publication may affect a reader's choice to engage with a text, depending on the importance of currency to the task at hand. These elements are supported by the standard which asks students to note how a text presents information (e.g., sequentially, comparatively, causally), so as to better understand how the text is organized.

Production elements are best analyzed in the pre-reading stage and can be introduced by either the teacher or the librarian. Many middle-grade students will already have some familiarity with these elements but can still benefit from a lesson plan that allows them to identify which elements are present, where they are located in the work, and what, if any, effect they have on the reader's attitude about the work. Are they familiar with the author? Is the title enticing? Does it matter if the information in the work is old or new?

An examination of production elements in *Claudette Colvin* reveals that they are utilized in several places in the book, including the cover, the Cataloging in Publication (CIP) page, the title page, the spine, the back cover, and page headings throughout the main text. Isolating these elements allows readers to think about what is there and why, as well as what is missing and why. Teachers and librarians can also use these elements as a basis for teaching the parts of a book, and such concepts as edition, copyright, and intellectual property.

Navigational

Navigational elements assist readers in understanding the organization of a work and how to search its content. With navigational elements, students can determine the central ideas or information of a primary or secondary source, provide an accurate summary of the source distinct from prior knowledge or opinions, and become familiar with how a text presents information (e.g., sequentially, comparatively, causally). In considering the navigational elements of the book, the key questions to ask are: How is the information organized? How easy are these elements to use? These elements are supported by the standards which ask students to consider the central ideas of a source, describe how the text leads them as a reader through the information, and to integrate the visual texts into their reading.

Claudette Colvin includes a wealth of navigational elements. There are two main sections (called "parts" in the book); each is numbered, has a title, and contains one or more epigraphs. In addition, the chapters of the book reflect this same structure: each is numbered, has a title, and contains one or more epigraphs. The table of contents, which appears immediately after the dedication page and immediately before Part 1, lists the two parts and the ten chapters, along with their section/chapter numbers, titles, and the page numbers on which they begin. In addition, the epilogue and its title are listed, as well as the nine elements that appear in the book's back matter.

One of the elements listed is the index, another important navigational tool. The index is seven and a half pages in length and is organized in the conventional way indexes are organized: names, places, and things are listed in alphabetical order with the page numbers listed where these topics can be found in the book. If a page number refers to an image, the number is italicized. A quick look at the table of contents reveals the main topics covered in the book and indicates the overall structure. A closer look at each section and chapter heading, including the epigraphs, provides additional information about the topics. The index provides even more detail. Thus, these navigational elements help readers not only to find their way around in the book, but also promote an understanding of the main ideas as well as how the book is put together.

Pre-reading and PLF in Action

As a pre-reading strategy, examining the table of contents (could also be completed with an index) can help readers understand how the book is organized and what topics are covered. Often a favorite reading strategy of content area teachers (Barry, 2002; Gallavan & Kottler, 2007; Moorf & Readence, 1984), visual organizers provide students with a way to synthesize their thinking, ask questions about what they are reading, and make predictions about what lies ahead within the text.

Using the table of contents as a prediction starter prepares students for the reading path ahead. Using a KWL chart as a self-monitoring tool, students can describe the background knowledge they have about the Civil Rights Movement, encouraging critical thinking and ownership in the learning by making a list of what they want to know as they move forward into the during-reading phase. Students can grapple with the many questions they likely have, including who was arrested and why. This self-selected visual organizer can assist students in their reading while also allowing for the flexibility of learning things they didn't know already about Claudette Colvin. Using this pre-reading tool during the reading of the text will guide students to pay attention to chapter titles and epigraphs that can help clarify the topics and main ideas of each chapter.

WHILE READING *CLAUDETTE COLVIN: TWICE TOWARD JUSTICE*

The during-reading phase can be used to assist students in considering the author's purpose, both in content and structural intent; making inferences; using context clues to tackle difficult vocabulary; making summarizations and generalizations; and connecting the text to other texts and world ideas, people, and events. This stage of reading also guides students into further inquiry, helping students to consider the value of the sources and evidence cited and building a capacity for gathering and evaluating resources. These functions also move students to continue to draw conclusions, make informed decisions based on their conclusions, and share their knowledge as members of a democratic society.

Supplemental

Supplemental elements guide the reader to a deeper comprehension of the text. Supplemental elements such as pictures, endpapers, photographs, tables, and timelines help authors illustrate their point of view, strengthen their arguments, and draw the reader to additional information that layers the complexity of the ideas presented. These elements are supported by the standards, which ask students to determine the meaning of words, consider the author's point of view, integrate visual texts, analyze primary and secondary documents, and read and comprehend texts independently and proficiently.

Pictures encompass a large portion of the supplemental text in *Claudette Colvin*. Throughout each chapter, pictures illustrate for the reader the real events described by Colvin and others. From the segregated bus picture at the beginning of chapter 1, to the classroom picture on p. 13, to the police report filed in 1955 on p. 35, each layer of photographs adds to the complexity of the text. It helps create a mind movie for the adolescent reader, many of whom have never experienced segregation in their lives. The captions on the pictures themselves offer a snapshot of what's to come within the text. Although an actual timeline does not exist, the pictures are displayed in the order of Claudette's story, creating a timeline of sorts.

PLF in Action while Reading

As an individual activity transitioning to a whole-class activity, the photographs within the text provide many opportunities for critical thinking. While reading, ask students to select a historical photograph contained within the text and complete a questioning brainstorm. After working independently, students then discuss in small groups the picture they selected and why, including their most important questions. After sharing out from groups, students offer their suggestions for a class-wide selection of a photograph to annotate together, which Daniels and Zemelman (2014) refer to as "the mother of all during-reading strategies" (p. 121).

Once the students have selected a photograph from the chapter, students can transfer the skills they used in their independent work to a digital annotation activity using ThingLink. Teachers know the importance of offering students the opportunity to analyze an extensive range of print and nonprint text and to encourage students to make multiliteracy connections within social media and Internet spaces (Hagood, 2012; Leu, Kinzer, Coiro, & Cammack, 2004;

Claudette Colvin Has Been Arrested

Roles:

Robert Clare: Bus Driver

Claudette Colvin: 15-year-old girl

Paul Headley: Police Officer

T.J. Ward: Police Officer

[Enter Officers Headley and Ward]

OFFICER PAUL HEADLEY: (To bus driver, angry)

What have we got this time? Who is it?

ROBERT CLARE: (Pointing directly at Claudette)

It's *her*! That's nothing new… I've had trouble with that *thing* before.

Figure 7.1.   Sample dramatic script

New London Group, 1996; Turner & Hicks, 2015). Collaboratively, students can annotate (insert questions and comments) in real time on the photograph, identifying additional resources, textual evidence, and even other cultural connections, including music using the "Digital Annotation of Rosa Parks/E.D. Nixon Photograph." By thinking aloud together in online spaces, students are also building metacognition individually and strengthening their own independent thinking (Daniels & Steineke, 2011; Harvey & Goudvis, 2007).

Another approach to using supplemental functions from the PLF is to highlight the primary sources illustrated within the chapter. Using the Claudette Colvin arrest record, students can be asked to bring the document to life by creating a dramatic script (see figure 7.1) based on the information it contains (Morris, 2001; Newmann, 1990).

AFTER READING *CLAUDETTE COLVIN: TWICE TOWARD JUSTICE*

After-reading strategies guide students to use what they have learned to make textual connections, interpret findings, outline or summarize information, and apply their knowledge. Application of knowledge allows students to become responsible citizens who collaborate with other people to find solutions to problems, reflect on their own actions, and influence societal change. These functions also move students to share their knowledge as members of a democratic society and to pursue personal growth.

Intratextual

Intratextual elements serve to interface between the work and the reader, often describing the author's process of researching and writing the work and acknowledging the assistance of others. Understanding the intratextual elements of a book can help promote an author's point of view or purpose. These elements are supported by standards which ask students to consider the author's point of view or purpose.

Two intratextual elements in *Claudette Colvin* that serve to thank or acknowledge other people for inspiring the book and/or assisting with the production of the book are the dedication (not labeled), which appears in the front matter just before the table of contents; and the "Acknowledgments" section, which appears in the back matter between the "Notes" and the "Picture Credits." Two other intratextual elements in the book serve to provide more context for the creation of the book and reflection on the story. In the "Author's Note," Hoose explains how he came to hear about Colvin's story, how he tracked her down, and how he conducted research for the book. The "Afterword," which was written expressly for the paperback edition of the book, presents an interview Hoose conducted with Colvin after the publication of the hardback version. Here Colvin describes her life as an adult and also talks about the effect the book's publication has had on her. In both the "Author's Note" and the "Afterword," Hoose's fascination with and attitude toward his subject are clearly foregrounded.

Although the intratextual elements can certainly be examined at any point in the reading process, with this particular book the intratextual elements may prove most useful at the post-reading stage. Once students have read the book, they can read the "Author's Note" and gain a greater understanding of what inspired the book and how the research was conducted. By examining the "Acknowledgments," they can find out who else contributed to the research and publication processes. And by reading the "Afterword," they can gain more information about the adult Claudette Colvin and her experiences since the book's initial publication. Again, all of these elements can be examined before reading the book as well as while reading the book, but they are likely to be most useful if examined afterwards.

Documentary

Documentary elements help the reader understand the origin or source of the information. As a reader, we have the opportunity to decide whether a source is legitimate and unbiased. Documentary elements provide the reader with a map of the author's thinking and research. These elements ask students to make reasoned judgments between fact and opinion and to consider the information from both primary and secondary sources.

The "Picture Credits" also add a layer of complexity, as readers can cross-reference from this for research or additional enrichment. For example, in examining why this story is not better known, students can search for other evidence that Claudette's story is true as well as evidence that other young people have had a hand in historical events, but may not have received recognition for their efforts.

After Reading and the PLF in Action

Creating digital texts based on the reading encourages students to model twenty-first-century skills. By using editorial cartoons, modeled as mentor texts from other editorial cartoons shared in class, teachers can offer students an opportunity to experiment with visual argument, persuasion, and debate as well as provide a visual interpretation of their thinking about the text (Bickford, 2016; Pescatore, 2007). For example, students that are allowed options in their assessments may choose to use editorial cartoons to focus on the intratextual function of the Author's Note and Afterword (see figure 7.2).

In addition, during the after-reading stage, students may wish to combine their understanding of the multiple functions of the Peritextual Literacy Framework. Ask students to work collaboratively to design potential ways to promote the novel, creating alternative book covers, a movie trailer for a potential motion picture, or designing a promotional poster of a hypothetical movie based on the text.

Figure 7.2.   Sample editorial cartoon

EXTENSION ACTIVITIES BEYOND *CLAUDETTE COLVIN: TWICE TOWARD JUSTICE*

Watch the *Claudette Colvin: Twice toward Justice* Video (3:27)

On the Macmillan website, the author talks about his research and students can hear the adult Claudette talk about her experience. Note: There is also a down loadable teacher's guide.

Create Text Sets

Find scaffolding texts on the Civil Rights Movement, Claudette Colvin, and other figures. Two excellent resources to use to accomplish this task: Newsela.com, which provides teachers the opportunity to organize text sets based on reading levels; and by exploring Coretta Scott King Awards, given in honor of the accomplishments of Dr. Martin Luther King and is wife Coretta Scott King in their work for peace. The award, given since 1970, showcases books that celebrate "African American culture and universal human values."

Other Unsung Heroes

Through primary sources, identify other "unsung heroes" of the Civil Rights Movement to tell their stories.

Oral Histories

Reach out to community members who lived during the Civil Rights Movement and record their stories in an Oral Histories project.

Family Literacy Night

Hold a Family Literacy Night to introduce auto-ethnographies and ways of documenting our own lives for the benefit of future generations

CONCLUSION

The Peritextual Literacy Framework offers social studies teachers an effective scaffold to integrate YA biographies into the curriculum. Offering connections to pre-reading, during-reading, and after-reading activities, the PLF in tandem with Claudette Colvin, can strengthen students' use of information and inquiry.

Social studies teachers who are reluctant to use YA nonfiction in the classroom can work collaboratively with the school or public librarian. The librarian can assist you in many ways

- Help develop lesson plans and assignments on your topic;
- Deliver lessons on the usefulness and importance of production elements;
- Help supply resources such as

  - Primary documentation
  - Related readings
  - Related media and other internet resources;

- Teach online search strategies;
- Assist students in searching for evidence and related materials;
- Help with the integration of technology into lesson plans; and
- Assist with student evaluation.

Annotated List of Related YA Literature

The Watsons Go to Birmingham, 1963 by Christopher Paul Curtis (210 pp.)

The Watson's, worried about their son Bryon getting out of hand, take a car trip to Birmingham to visit Grandma. During their visit, their church is blown up.

We Were There Too!: Young People in U.S. History by Philip M. Hoose (276 pp.)

Hoose documents the participation of young people in American History beginning with Columbus' voyage and demonstrates the important role young people can play as activists. History isn't only about adults.

REFERENCES

Alsup, J. (2013). Teaching literature in an age of text complexity. *Journal of Adolescent & Adult Literacy, 57*(3), 181–184.

Assembly on Literature for Adolescents of the NCTE (ALAN) (2016). *ALAN Foundation Grant*. Retrieved from http://www.alan-ya.org/awards/alan-foundation-grant/.

Barry, A. L. (2002). Reading strategies teachers say they use. *Journal of Adolescent & Adult Literacy, 46*(2), 132–141.

Bickford, J. H. (2016). Integrating creative, critical, and historical thinking through close reading, document-based writing, and original political cartooning. *The Councilor: A Journal of the Social Studies, 77*(1), 1–9.

Blasingame, J. (2007). *Books that don't bore 'em.* New York: Scholastic.

Carlson, R. G. (1980). *Books and the teen-age reader.* New York: Harper & Row.

Curtis, C. P. (2000). *The Watsons Go to Birmingham, 1963.* New York: Laurel Leaf.

Daniels, H., & Steineke, N. (2011). *Texts and lessons for content-area reading.* Portsmouth, NH: Heinemann.

Daniels, H., & Zemelman, S. (2014). *Subjects matter: Exceeding standards through powerful content-area reading.* Portsmouth, NH: Heinemann.

Dobbs, C. L., Ippolito, J., & Charner-Laird, M. (2016). Layering intermediate and disciplinary literacy work: Lessons learned from a secondary social studies teacher team. *Journal of Adolescent & Adult Literacy, 60*(2), 131–139.

Gallavan, N. P., & Kottler, E. (2007). Eight types of graphic organizers for empowering social studies students and teachers. *The Social Studies, 98*(3), 117–128.

Genette, G. (1997). *Paratexts: Thresholds of interpretation.* New York: Cambridge University Press.

Groenke, S., & Scherff, L. (2010). *Teaching YA lit through differentiated instruction.* Urbana, IL: National Council of Teachers of English.

Guthrie, J. T., & Coddington, C. S. (2009). Reading motivation. In K. R. Wentzel & A. Wigfield (Eds.), *Handbook of motivation at school*, 503–525. New York: Routledge.

Hagood, M. C. (2012). Risks, rewards, and responsibilities of using new literacies in middle grades. *Voices from the Middle, 19*(4), 10–16.

Harvey, S., & Goudvis, A. (2007). *Strategies that work: Teaching comprehension for understanding and engagement.* Portland, ME: Stenhouse Publishers.

Hayes, D. A., & R. J. Tierney. (1982). Developing readers' knowledge through analogy. *Reading Research Quarterly, 17*(2), 256–280.

Hoose, P M. (2001). *We were there too!: Young people in U.S. History.* New York: Farrar, Straus and Giroux.

Hoose, P. M. (2009). *Claudette Colvin: Twice toward justice.* New York: Melanie Kroupa Books/Farrar Straus Giroux.

Lafferty, K. E. (2014). What are you reading? How school libraries can promote racial diversity in multicultural literature. *Multicultural Perspectives, 16*(4), 203–209.

Lesesne, T. (2003). *Making the match: The right book for the right reader at the right time.* Portland, ME: Stenhouse.

Leu, D. J., Kinzer, C. K., Coiro, J. L., & Cammack, D. W. (2004). Toward a theory of new literacies emerging from the Internet and other information and communication technologies. In N. J. Unrau & R. B. Ruddell (Eds.), *Theoretical models and processes of reading* (5th ed.), 1570–1613. Newark, DE: International Reading Association. Retrieved from http://www.reading.org/downloads/publications/books/bk502-54-Leu.pdf.

Marinak, B., & Gambrell, L. (2009). Ways to teach about informational text. *Social Studies and the Young Learner, 22*(1), 19–22.

Miller, D. (2013). *Reading in the wild: The book whisperers' keys to cultivating lifelong reading habits.* San Francisco, CA: Jossey-Bass.

Moorf, D. W., & Readence, J. F. (1984). A quantitative and qualitative review of graphic organizer research. *The Journal of Educational Research, 78*(1), 11–17.

Morris, R. V. (2001). Drama and authentic assessment in a social studies classroom. *The Social Studies, 92*(1), 41–44.

New London Group (1996). A pedagogy of multiliteracies: Designing social futures. *Harvard Educational Review, 66*(1), 60–92.

Newmann, F. M. (1990). Higher order thinking in teaching social studies: A rationale for the assessment of classroom thoughtfulness. *Journal of Curriculum Studies, 22*(1), 41–56.

Partnership for 21st Century Skills (2009). *P21 framework definitions.* Retrieved from http://www.p21.org/storage/documents/P21_Framework_Definitions.pdf.

Pescatore, C. (2007). Current events as empowering literacy: For English and social studies teachers. *Journal of Adolescent & Adult Literacy, 51*(4), 326–339.

Sheffield, C. C., Chisholm, J. S., & Howell, P. B. (2015). Graphic novels and multi-modal literacy in social studies education. *Social Education, 79*(3), 147–150.

Thinglink. Digital annotation of Rosa Parks/E.D. *Nixon photograph.* Retrieved from https://www.thinglink.com/scene/837776542305091585.

Turner, K. H., & Hicks, T. (2015). *Connected reading: Teaching adolescent readers in a digital world.* Urbana, IL: National Council of Teachers of English.

Vacca, J., & Vacca, R. (1999). *Content area reading: Literacy and learning across the curriculum* (6th ed.). New York: Longman.

Waters, S., & Jenkins, L. (2015). Young adult historical fiction in the middle grades social studies classroom: Can literature increase student interest and test scores? *Learning and Teaching, 8*(2), 39–61.

Young, T. A., Moss, B., & Cornwell, L. (2007). The classroom library: A place for nonfiction, nonfiction in its place. *Reading Horizons, 48*(1), 1–18.

Chapter 8

Introducing Students to the Background of the Civil Rights Movement by Using *Mississippi Trial, 1955*

Katie Irion and Chris Crowe

On May 17, 1954, in the landmark *Brown vs. the Board of Education* case, the Supreme Court ruled that state laws establishing separate public schools for black and white students were unconstitutional. The decision sparked a riot of backlash and set many people on edge in the already fractious South. On August 28, 1955, little more than a year after this historic verdict, a Chicago teenager named Emmett Till was kidnaped, tortured, and murdered in the Mississippi Delta. His death and the subsequent trial of his murderers shocked the nation and helped spark the modern Civil Rights Movement.

At a storefront in Money, Mississippi, fourteen-year-old Till whistled at a white woman. When her husband and brother-in-law found out, they kidnaped him from his uncle's home, and with the help of several others, tortured and murdered him then disposed of his body in the Tallahatchie River. To the surprise of most local residents, the two men were arrested and put on trial, but after five days, an all-white jury pronounced them not guilty of murder. The resulting outrage over this injustice ignited a growing civil rights movement and compelled many people, including Rosa Parks and Martin Luther King, Jr., to speak out and stand up against racism.

This chapter highlights the Emmett Till case through the use of the young adult (YA) novel *Mississippi Trial, 1955* (Crowe, 2003a). This story, told through the eyes of fictional Hiram Hillburn, will serve as a springboard to discuss the historical context, racial tensions, and ideology that existed during this time period.

MISSISSIPPI TRIAL, 1955 BY CHRIS CROWE (231 PP.)

Hiram has nothing but fond memories of his home in Mississippi. For the first eight years of his life, he lived with his grandparents in Greenwood and loved spending his days fishing, going on walks, exploring nature, and idolizing his grandfather. When his parents moved him to Arizona, he missed Mississippi and his grandfather desperately.

Now, almost 16, Hiram is back in Mississippi to spend the summer with Grampa. Initially he is excited, but before long, his excitement wears off, and he begins to feel like the Mississippi of his youth is more complex than he remembered. He meets a fourteen-year-old African American boy visiting from Chicago named Emmett Till and begins to see how African Americans are treated by the white citizens of Greenwood. Hiram begins to question the racist traditions of his community, but he finds no solace in Grampa, a man who fiercely believes in the "southern way" of life and considers segregation essential to the preservation of American society.

When Emmett's mutilated corpse is found floating in the Tallahatchie River, Hiram is convinced that his older friend, R. C. Rydell, is somehow involved. To the surprise of everyone in town, a trial is announced; Hiram attends with his grandfather and witnesses firsthand the stunning reality of racial injustice. After the trial, Hiram's idealized view of the South and his grandfather are irrevocably altered, and he leaves Greenwood with a new perspective on race, friendship, justice, and hate.

CONNECTING HISTORY AND LITERACY

In this chapter, the reading of *Mississippi Trial, 1955* is housed within a unit on the American Civil Rights Movement. Through the study of this novel, students will be able to analyze why the death of Emmett Till was one of the sparks that ignited the modern Civil Rights Movement. Students can discuss and write about events that contributed to the death of Emmett Till, including Jim Crow laws and *Brown vs. The Board of Education*. By the end, students will have improved their historical literacy, which is their ability to read, write, and think critically about the past, and will be able to identify and critique primary and secondary sources relevant to this historical moment.

BEFORE READING *MISSISSIPPI TRIAL, 1955*

To help students achieve the greatest comprehension of the literature, a day or two devoted to pre-reading strategies is essential. According to Boling and Evans (2008), the pre-reading technique serves two purposes: first, it establishes the purpose for reading and second, it activates the students' prior knowledge of the topic. Students read for a variety of reasons. They read to perform a task, to have a literary experience, and to be informed. Establishing a premise for why they are reading allows students the opportunity to discover why reading needs to occur (Tovani, 2000). An essential component of pre-reading instruction is the activation of the students' prior knowledge. In the World War II example, pictures, memorabilia, and music may help students recall information about the topic. With their background knowledge stimulated, students are ready to attach new information to existing knowledge (Anderson, 1977). These connections facilitate comprehension and lead to reading success (pp. 60–61).

There is a direct correlation to pre-reading strategies and reading success, comprehension, and understanding. *Mississippi Trial, 1955* requires basic knowledge of the Civil Rights era and Jim Crow laws in order to be fully appreciated and understood. Emmett Till's murder was facilitated and supported by the laws that protected white people. Students' comprehension of the novel will increase when they know about the Jim Crow laws that existed during this time period. Before students begin reading the novel, take some time to conduct a brief discussion of Jim Crow in the 1950s. Ask students to name some key political and public figures from that era.

Have students increase their knowledge of primary and secondary sources by dividing students into groups. Give each group an article about life during the Jim Crow era and have students read their article and then complete three tasks: (1) summarize the article, (2) predict what happens next, and (3) present their article and predication to the class. As a class, make a timeline of the important, historical events that shaped the Civil Rights Movement. A great resource for this exploration can be found at PBS "The Rise and Fall of Jim Crow Intergenerational Discussion Guide."

Emmett Till plays a central role, not only in the novel *Mississippi Trial, 1955*, but also in the historical timeline of our country. His death forced the country to have a conversation about the treatment of African American people. He is a central figure in the Civil Rights Movement, and students should have a basic understanding about him as a historical figure. A lesson discussing the real life of Emmett Till will serve students well before they read about him in the novel. Show students a photo of Emmett Till and have them respond to the following prompts: What assumptions might you make just by looking at this picture? How do you think this boy figures into history? Once students have written or discussed their predictions about Emmett Till give some brief background of Till's murder, then, in pairs, have students use a KWL chart to list what they know about Emmett Till, and what they want to learn about him. Tell students that they are going to be reading about the time when Emmett was murdered, and give a few facts about Emmett Till that students might find pertinent and interesting. Then, introduce students to *Mississippi Trial, 1955* by reading aloud the first six paragraphs of the novel.

In conjunction with this prediction activity and discussion about Emmett Till, consider using an activity that helps students compare and contrast different perspectives about the same topic. Have students read and listen to the songs "The Death of Emmett Till" by Bob Dylan (1972) and "My Name is Emmett Till" by Emmy Lou Harris (2010). Give students a copy of the lyrics, and after they have listened to the songs and read the lyrics have them answer the following questions about each song, either in a small-group discussion or on their own:

• Who is Emmett Till?
• What do you think this song is based on?
• What happens to Emmett Till in this song? Why?
• What time period do you think Emmett Till lived in? What leads you to think this?
• What happened to the men who hurt Emmett Till?
• What are Dylan and Harris' opinions about the justice system?
• Why do these singers want people to remember this incident?
• One line in Dylan's song, written in 1962, is, "This kind of thing still lives today." Does this line still apply to us today? Why or why not?

Take some time to compare and contrast both artists' point of view.

Much of our history is based on personal accounts from people who lived during certain times or witnessed historic events. In order to have a better understanding of the time period that Emmett Till lived in and to help determine the meaning of words and phrases as they are used in a text, including political aspects of history, have students read personal accounts about what it was like to live during the time that Emmett Till lived. Have students read authentic accounts and discuss what life was like for young people during the time Emmett Till was alive. Discuss differences they are able to pinpoint. Also, discuss how the accounts differ from what they read about in history books. Which is the "true" history? Public Broadcasting Service (PBS) is an excellent online resource for locating these primary documents under the heading "Teens and Segregation."

One such reality that many African Americans had to live with during this time period was lynching. Students today may or may not know what this term means, and in order to fully understand the history in this time period, students must be familiar with this term and its history. Read with students about lynching in America; PBS has "People and Events: Lynching in America" that can help with this. Lynchings often were public events, and photographs of lynching victims were published in newspapers and on postcards. Have students imagine they are an African American living in the South and have them write a letter to a friend describing their reaction to hearing about a recent lynching in their area and seeing photographs of it. What emotions does this create for them? How might it affect future behavior?

Brown vs. The Board of Education is a landmark case in American legal history and is referenced repeatedly in *Mississippi Trial, 1955*. The understanding of the importance of this case is imperative to understanding the angst and anger that many characters in the book feel. Also, important is *Brown II*. In May 1955, the Supreme Court unanimously approved *Brown II*, which instructed states to begin desegregation plans "with all deliberate speed." Discuss with the class the ruling from the Supreme Court and what that meant for American schools. View a map from the U.S. Census Bureau showing the population density of African Americans across the United States in 1950. If schools were forced to be desegregated, how would the white populations be affected, particularly in the South?

To help students achieve historical literacy, they need to have a knowledge of historical sources. Students should understand the difference between primary and secondary sources in order to analyze *Mississippi Trial, 1955*'s sources, including its use of primary sources—the articles from *The Greenwood Commonwealth*. This discussion is a great springboard for further discussions when students are in the middle of reading the book. Using images and articles, teach students about primary and secondary sources and how they shape history. Before students come to class, cover the classroom with primary and secondary sources from any period in history. Send the students, in pairs, on a hunt. Number each source and give each student a numbered piece of paper. Instruct students to walk around the classroom, read each source and decide among themselves if the source is primary or secondary. Once students have read all the sources, review them with the class and ask students the value of each type of source. Ask students how the sources shape history.

Show students "When One Mother Defied America: The Photo that Changed the Civil Rights Movement" (*Time*, 2016) a video (8:29) that uses interviews and film footage from the Emmett Till case will provide important historical context as students continue their reading of the text.

WHILE READING *MISSISSIPPI TRIAL, 1955*

To make it easier for teachers to find activities that pertain to certain sections of the novel, this section is divided into three segments: first third of book, second third, and final third. This section suggests things teachers can do to help their students comprehend the novel and its historical context. The activities that are presented utilize many different reading strategies in order to facilitate the most learning and comprehension among all learning styles. Many of the activities build upon what students learned while completing lessons in the pre-reading section. McLaughlin (2012) observes, "Meaning is constructed when readers make connections between what they know (prior knowledge) and what they are reading (the text)" (432). The activities also incorporate core standards that enhance students' historical literacy such as analyzing a series of events in a text, determining meaning of words and phrases in the text, analyzing structure of a text to emphasize key points, and assessing author's claims.

First Third of the Novel (pp. 1–76)

The first third of *Mississippi Trial, 1955* introduces readers to the setting, the key characters, and the themes that impact the book's plot. One of the major themes is the complicated nature of father-son relationships. Hiram doesn't agree with his father's attitudes, just as Hiram's father struggles with Grampa's attitudes. This tension is discussed from the first page of the book and heavily influences Hiram's worldview. His view of the world shifts dramatically from the first page to the end of the story, and discussing Hiram's attitudes and beliefs and how they are shaped by both his father and his grandfather is imperative to understanding the theme of prejudice in the novel.

After students have read the first third of the novel, instead of relying on a study guide or worksheet, use class time to discuss the role of fathers in the story and how their views affect other characters. Discussion is the better strategy because there is a level of comprehension that follows discussion of questions that is not always achieved by simply writing down answers. In their study of how discussion influences reading, Hurst and Pearman (2013) conclude that "students learn more when they are able to talk to one another and be actively involved" (p. 228). They quote Routman's explanation that "talking with others about what we read increases our understanding. Collaborative talk is a powerful way to make meaning" (p. 228) and then summarize that "providing daily opportunities for students to read and interact with texts and each other is an important component of any class" (p. 228). The following prompts may help frame productive classroom discussions:

- On the first page of *Mississippi Trial, 1955*, Hiram tells us something interesting about his father. He says, "My father hates hate." What do we learn about Hiram's father in the first seven chapters that supports this statement? Write down some things Dad or Hiram say that support this statement.
- What do you think life was like for Hiram's father in Mississippi when he was growing up?
- What historical figures might have influenced his thinking? Knowing what you know about Jim Crow, what was life like for African Americans in Mississippi while Hiram's father was growing up?
- Is Dad's opinion about hate similar to his father's and neighbors' or different?

Have students read first-hand accounts of what life was life for teenagers living in this time period, in this region of America and discuss what they learn. PBS offers students these resources: "Mississippi Then, Mississippi Now"; "Sex and Race"; and "People and Events: Citizen's Councils."

When Hiram arrives in Mississippi, he immediately notices differences from Arizona. Lead a class discussion about what Hiram notices and why he notices those things. Place students in groups and have them create a T-comparison chart, with one column filled with details about how Ruthanne acts and the other column with how Bobo/Emmett Till acts. Ask the students to draw some conclusions about the differences between the two characters. Does this say anything about how African Americans were treated in the South versus the North? Scenes like this one are not documented in history but were written by the author for the sake of the novel. Why would the author write this particular scene? Where did Crowe get the idea that Emmett Till was not a typical southern African American? Have students read articles describing Emmett Till and have them infer about his personality and disposition, just as Crowe did to write this scene; a good resource is Emmett Till's Bio at biography.com. Allow students to assess the extent to which reasoning and evidence in a text supports Crowe's representations.

Literacy research suggests that reading success and high comprehension in the social sciences is enhanced when students understand new vocabulary. After studying the effects of vocabulary on reading, Nitzskin, Katzir, and Sulkind (2014) concluded that "vocabulary had the highest correlation to reading comprehension" (p. 31). Hiram discovers that Grampa is heavily involved with the White Citizens' Council and Council meetings. The term *council* may be new to most students, so understanding what the word means and what it implied is imperative to the understanding of the text and the time period. Spend a class period researching and figuring out what the Council is. Why does the author capitalize the word "Council"? If students have access to a computer, assign them to work in pairs to research and define a list of key terms that appear in the novel or that are related to this historical period (e.g., Klu Klux Klan, Jim Crow, racial segregation, White Citizen's Council, Black Monday, white supremacy, and NAACP). If computers are not available, provide students these words and their definitions and/or historical context and have students highlight and summarize important facts and then present the word or term, with a relevant explanation, to the class.

Middle Third of the Novel (pp. 77–145)

The middle third section of *Mississippi Trial, 1955* follows Hiram as he encounters Emmett Till. In this section, Emmett Till is murdered, and the ramifications from that heinous act unfold. Till's case is well documented, and while some pictures are graphic, it would be beneficial for students to visualize the key events of the case. Hurst and Pearman (2013) report that "teaching students to visualize what they are reading can help them improve their comprehension of the text" (p. 228). There is a collection of photos from the Till case that would be beneficial to show students. Show students the photos and discuss whether or not the historical images are what they had visualized from reading the novel. Photos can be retrieved by searching under the heading "Pictures from 1955—Emmett Till Murder."

When Grampa is talking to Hiram, he often includes mention of "the southern way of life." Building on what students know from their pre-reading work, ask them what they think Grampa means by "the southern way of life." For example, Grampa was especially upset about the Supreme Court's *Brown vs. the Board of Education* decision. Why would that decision bother him so much, and what sort of lifestyle is Grampa referring to? Many of conflicts during this time period resulted from the debate about States' rights. People like Grampa wanted the States to have more rights because that would allow local government to manage—and mainly restrict—the freedom of African Americans. Extend students' understanding of this historical period and its role in the novel by discussing the Tenth Amendment. Be sure to point out that the Tenth Amendment is still relevant in today's political environment, just as it was in the 1950s. This discussion will help students connect the past to the present. Have students research some secondary sources that discuss states' rights in our present day. "States' Rights Arguments Can't Be Sepa-rated from History" (Doolittle, 2017) is an informative article about States' rights and how they have been viewed in the past and how they're still the basis for political wrangling today.

Mississippi Trial, 1955 provides a window into what life may have been like for African Americans in the South in the 1950s. When Hiram and R.C. go fishing, they run into Emmett and some of his friends. What unfolds after Hiram offers Emmett the leftovers from his lunch is a difficult scene to read, but it provides valuable historical context for students to consider. Using pas-sages from the text, find examples of how R.C. treats Emmett. What attitude does R.C. display toward Emmett and his cousins? At one point in this scene, R.C. says, "I've had enough of your uppityness" (p. 91). Have students write down what they think R.C. meant by that comment, and then discuss their responses as a class.

Final Third of the Novel (pp. 155–229)

The final third of *Mississippi Trial, 1955* shows what Hiram does during the trial of Till's murderers, and most importantly, how he reacts to the trial and how it changes him. When students have finished the book, they should have the opportunity to discuss the characters and how they changed and/

or remained static. Students can connect to the characters by completing an identity chart for one of the characters in the novel. The website, "Facing History and Ourselves" describes the purpose of this assignment: "Identity charts are a graphic tool that helps students consider the many factors that shape who we are as individuals and as communities. They can be used to deepen students' understanding of themselves, groups, nations and historical and literary figures. Sharing . . . Identity charts with peers can help students build relationships."

After explaining how to complete this assignment, give students time to select a character from the novel and then complete an identity chart of their own. When they have finished, provide an opportunity to discuss what they discovered in small groups or as a class. This will not only allow students to identify with a character in a more personal way, but will also help them analyze a series of events described in the text through a character's eyes (9–10.3).

In the novel, Crowe devotes several chapters to the actual trial of Emmett's killers. Readers get to see the trial through Hiram's eyes, but at the time, most Americans were reading about it in newspapers and magazines. Three months after the murder trial, the defendants Roy Bryant and J. W. Milam, gave an interview to *Look* magazine and confessed to killing Emmett Till. That interview by William Bradford Huie (1956) called, "The Shocking Story of Approved Killing in Mississippi" is a primary source that provides students with a firsthand account of a prominent historical moment. Students can determine the central ideas of information of a primary source while discussing how history played out in "reality" per Bryant and Milam, and in fiction in Crowe's book. Have students read the interview and then discuss their conclusions about it. Lead a class discussion about "double jeopardy" and the legal system in America. Is justice always "fair"? In the *Look* article, Huie mentions multiple times that this is "the truth." Do newspapers and magazines always publish the "truth"? How can readers detect bias in a media account?

The confession from the two murderers in *Look* magazine provoked many readers to express their opinions about the article, and many of those opinions are available to read. Have students read the Letters to the Editor and consider these questions: Why were people upset? Why were some reactions positive? Where did the authors of those letters live? What correlation might exist between regions of the United States and different attitudes expressed in the letters? After reading a handful of letters from ordinary, everyday citizens, discuss how two people can respond the same event in completely different opinions.

Students may be interested in looking at the Federal Bureau of Investigations (FBI)'s report on its investigation on the Emmett Till case that includes an autopsy report and a copy of the long-lost trial transcripts. Callard's 2009 interview with Simeon Wright, one of Emmett Till's cousins who was in the house when Emmett was kidnapped, should also stimulate interest.

AFTER READING *MISSISSIPPI TRIAL, 1955*

Students' comprehension is not finished when the last page of the *Mississippi Trial, 1955* is over. In order to solidify their learning, students need post-reading activities that require analysis and summary. Cox (2017), in discussing post reading activities, observes that "after or post-reading strategies provide students a way to summarize, reflect, and question what they have just read" (par. 1) thus improving comprehension and retention.

When the class has finished reading *Mississippi Trial, 1955*, students will be prepared to use the knowledge from the text and from the primary and secondary sources they've studied in pre- and during-reading activities to discuss and analyze the novel and the historical facts about Emmett Till's death in a historical context. Fortunately, there is a rich historical record that documents this famous case. The murder of Emmett Till and the subsequent trial of Roy Bryant and J. W. Milam spurred many people to put pen to paper. Some thought that the FBI should get involved in the case, while others directed letters of criticism or praise toward the district attorney who had prosecuted the case. State and federal politicians, including President Dwight Eisenhower, received letters about the case (see PBS Primary Sources: Reactions in Writing). Have students read the following letters written after the trial, and then have them answer the following questions:

- What is the general reaction to the case?
- What did most people want to happen?
- Who were there people who were happy with the result of the trial? Why do you think they were pleased?
- Do Americans have a right to express their opinion even if it is filled with negative or racist remarks? Why or why not?
- Based on the content of these letters, what do you think race relations were like during this time period?

These questions not only help students summarize the general outcry and/or support at Emmett Till's death but also help them analyze the series of events describe in the novel.

Every classroom has many different types of learners; some are auditory or kinesthetic, while others are read-write or visual learners. One effective way to reach visual learners, and to help them solidify the material they were reading, is to spend a class period watching the PBS documentary *The Murder of Emmett Till*. This extremely informational and well-researched documentary is a great review of the historical content of *Mississippi Trial, 1955,* and it allows students time to process the information they have studied and read about. In order to facilitate directed learning, have students keep a journal while they watch and have them note anything from the documentary that is different from the book. When the film is finished, have students answer the following questions, either individually or as a class: What is your initial reaction to this movie? What is one new thing you learned? What are some things from the film that were not mentioned in the novel? The book does a good job of describing what happened to Emmett Till, and during the reading you imagined those details, but how does the movie imagery affect you in a different way? Hiram and his grandfather are fictional characters, but what does reading about their perspective make you think about when you think of Emmett Till? Are there other "voices" from that time period you'd like to hear or know how they reacted?

Another type of learner that is often not addressed is the auditory learner. When you finish reading the novel, consider using songs as a way to reinforce historical literacy. Even if you used them in the pre-reading section, Emmylou Harris' and Bob Dylan's songs can serve as a good review of the time period. Have students listen to and read the lyrics to both songs again, and this time discuss whether or not they can be considered historical documents. Did either of them get facts wrong? Can we trust songs as forms of history? Look at the songs as a historian might, and discuss what historical details the song writers used and what is missing or lacking:

While studying history, students are sometimes stymied by the tension between nonfiction and historical fiction. How do historical accounts in textbooks differ from independent nonfiction fiction accounts of the same events? And in historical fiction, how can a reader know what's been sensationalized or fictionalized? *Mississippi Trial, 1955* is a good example of an historical novel. After reading the novel, have students discuss the difference between nonfiction and fiction. Writing the novel required Crowe to conduct a lot of historical research, but he still had to invent plot events to make the novel complete. Help students understand that good historians assess the extent to which historical evidence supports an author's claims in a novel. Have students look back through the book and write down specific things that Crowe invented for his novel. Discuss the following prompts with your students: What is the author's bias? What evidence in the book leads you to that conclusion? What parts of the story did the author take straight from history? This discussion help students think about primary and secondary sources. Have students find examples in the novel where Crowe may have used primary sources and examples of when he used secondary sources. Crowe's web page where he discusses the where *Mississippi Trial, 1955* came from is helpful to achieve this purpose.

Writing historical fiction allows authors to imagine and narrate emotional reactions to historical moments that may not be documented in textbooks and primary sources. Reading these emotional moments permits readers to connect to past events in ways they may not be able to by reading nonfiction. In *Mississippi Trial, 1955*, Chris Crowe wrote about Hiram's reaction to Emmett's death, and readers can understand how he felt. In order to have students connect to the time period and to a character from the novel, have them select a character from the book and write a journal entry about Emmett Till's death from that character's perspective. Some possible choices could be the following: Moses Wright, Carolyn Bryant, Naomi Rydell, Mr. Paul, or Mamie Till.

EXTENSION ACTIVITIES BEYOND *MISSISSIPPI TRIAL, 1955*

Poet Marilyn Nelson wrote a collection of poems about Emmett Till, his death, and how it changed people, including herself. She writes beautiful, poignant sonnets that reveal different emotions and reactions to Emmett Till's murder. As a class, read the poem, "Rosemary for remembrance, Shakespeare wrote," from *A Wreath for Emmett Till* (Nelson, 2005). This poem mentions many different flowers and the meaning and symbolism that each conveys. Teach students about the historical significance of flowers, and give them a glossary with flowers and plants and the meanings attached to each. Once students have familiarized themselves with the flowers and their meanings, have them design a wreath for Emmett Till by choosing the flowers and plants that best describe him and his experience. Allow students time to draw their wreath and then have them explain, either to the class or in small groups, the meanings behind what they chose and why.

In 1955, the prominent African American magazine, *Jet*, closely covered the trial of Emmett's murderers. One of the extraordinary and courageous aspects of their coverage was the inclusion of photos from the case, most notably the gruesome photographs of Emmett corpse. This raises some interesting points in documenting history: Are photos crucial to documenting history, and can they be considered primary documents? Have students read the first-hand accounts from young adults who lived in 1955 and who saw the photos in *Jet* magazine. Prepare famous photos from the civil rights movement and discuss as a class, or in small groups, the impact these photos may have had or continue to have on how people perceive historical events. Are photographs subjective? Do they speak the "truth?" Are they more reliable as a historical document than a journal entry or court document? Why or why not? Questions like these develop historical literacy by encouraging students to be critical thinkers.

Emmett Till never intended to be a leader in the Civil Rights Movement. He was just a fourteen-year-old boy visiting relatives in the summer of 1955, but his death fanned an already smoldering fire and prompted many people to stand up for their rights. In Montgomery, Alabama, less than 100 days after his murder, Rosa Parks refused to give up her seat on the bus to a white man. In explaining her act that led to the famous Montgomery Bus Boycott, Parks said, "I thought about Emmett Till, and I couldn't go back [to the back of the bus]." Of course, not all civil rights activists cite Emmett Till's murder as motivation for their protests, but history suggests that his brutal murder inspired many to stand up. Have students review a list of civil rights leaders who came to prominence after Emmett Till's death. Either with a group or as individuals, have students choose an activist to spotlight, and choose one of the following activities for students to complete:

Podcast

Create the conversation your civil rights activist and the podcast interviewer would have. Discuss background, likes and dislikes, goals, and experiences they have had.

Photographs

Find three or four photos that would have special significance to your activist. Mount them on a sheet of paper and explain why the pictures would mean something to your activist.

Poetry

Write three poems about your civil rights activist.

Journalism

Write a newspaper article as if you were living during the time your civil rights activist was doing something extraordinary.

Draw a Scene

If you are artistic, draw or paint a particular scene that would mean a lot to your leader. Explain what led up to that scene and the impact it had on your leader's life.

CONCLUSION

The murder of Emmett Till had a major impact on American society in 1955, but its influence continues even today (see textbox 8.1). There is so much to study that an entire course could be developed just on the case and its influence. We hope that the study suggestions here ignite your students' interests in history as well as develop their empathy to the plight of those Americans deemed "other" or "less than."

CHRONOLOGY OF TWENTY-FIRST-CENTURY DEVELOPMENTS IN THE CASE

January 5, 2003: Emmett's mother, Mamie Till Mobley, dies
January 19, 2003: PBS documentary airs
January–December 2004: documentarian Keith Beauchamp begins private screenings of "The Untold Story of Emmett Louis Till" and starts a petition campaign to reopen the case
April 11, 2004: artist Franklin McMahon donates his courtroom drawings from *Life* magazine to the Chicago Historical Society
May 10, 2004: U.S. Justice Department announces the case is reopened
October 24, 2004: "60 Minutes" feature on the case
May 4, 2005: exhumation and autopsy announced
May 18, 2005: copy of trial transcripts discovered
July 29, 2005: Henry Lee Loggins, 82, named possible accomplice in murder
August 28, 2005: Fiftieth anniversary of the kidnapping of Emmett Till
October 24, 2005: Rosa Parks dies
March 16, 2006: FBI announces that no federal charges will be filed
February 11, 2007: Mississippi schedules a Leflore County grand jury hearing to review evidence against Carolyn Bryant
February 27, 2007: Leflore County Grand Jury declines to indict Carolyn Bryant or anyone else
March 30, 2007: FBI releases results of investigation, including trial transcripts, online.
August 28, 2009: Emmett Till's casket to be displayed in the Smithsonian
January 14, 2014, Juanita Milam, wife of J. W. Milam, dies.

Annotated List of Related YA Literature

They Called Themselves the KKK by Susan Campbell Bartoletti (176 pp.)

This impressively researched book uses photographs, primary documents, and other sources to tell the story of the Ku Klux Klan from their beginnings into the twenty-first century.

Warriors Don't Cry: The Searing Memoir of the Battle to Integrate Little Rock's Central High by Melba Pattillo Beals (240 pp.)

In 1957, Beals and eight of her classmates were the first African American students to integrate Central High School in Little Rock, Arkansas. This first-person account of that year captures the courage, racism, and political fighting that surrounded the event.

The Story of Ruby Bridges by Robert Coles (32 pp.)

For younger readers, this book tells the story of Ruby Bridges, the six-year-old first grader who, in 1960, became the first African American to integrate a white school in New Orleans.

Getting away with Murder: The True Story of the Emmett Till Case by Chris Crowe (128 pp.)

In documentary style, using many photographs from the case, this book tells the full story of the Emmett Till murder case.

Ruby Lee and Me by Shannon Hitchcock (224 pp.)

Told by twelve-year-old Sarah Beth Willis, this is a story about change and questions. In 1969, schools were being integrated in the rural south. Sarah's not bothered by having the first black teacher ever in the rural South but is disturbed why she and Ruby Lee can't be best friends. The trouble is Sarah is white and Ruby is black.

Freedom's Children: Young Civil Rights Activists Tell Their Own Stories by Ellen S. Levine (192 pp.)

Thirty African Americans recount experiences related to their involvement in the Civil Rights Movement in their youth.

The Road to Memphis by Mildred D. Taylor (320 pp.)

This novel is the story of Cassie Logan, Taylor's protagonist in her Newbery Medal novel, *Roll of Thunder, Hear My Cry* in 1941 when she is seventeen years old. Her friends and family experience new kinds of racism, complicated by the start of World War II.

REFERENCES

Anderson, R. (1977). *The notion of schemata and the educational enterprise.* In R.C. Anderson, R.J. Spiro & W.E. Montague (eds.), Schooling and the Acquisition of Knowledge (pp. 415–431. Hillsdale, NJ: Lawrence Erlbaum Associates.

Bartoletti, S. C. (2014). *They called themselves the KKK*. Boston, MA: HMH Books for Young Readers.

Beals, M. P. (2007). *Warriors don't cry: The searing memoir of the battle to integrate Little Rock's Central High*. New York: Simon Pulse.

Boling, C. J., & Evans, W. H. (2008). Reading success in the secondary classroom. *Preventing School Failure, 52*(2), 59–66.

Callard, A. (2009). *Emmett Till's casket goes to the Smithsonian*. Retrieved from http://www.smithsonianmag.com/arts-culture/QA-Simeon-Wright.html.

Coles, R. (2010). *The story of Ruby Bridges*. New York: Scholastic Paperbacks.

Cox, J. (2017). Post reading teaching strategies. *Teach HUB*. Retrieved from http://www.teachhub.com/post-reading-teaching-strategies.

Crowe, C. (2003a). *Mississippi trial, 1955*. New York: Speak.

Crowe, C. (2003b). *Getting away with murder: The true story of the Emmett Till Case*. New York: Dial Books.

Doolittle, T. T. (2017). *States' rights arguments can't be separated from history*. Retrieved from http://www.statesman.com/news/opinion/states-rights-arguments-can-separated-from-history/qxKdzAchJlQU1qpgENeySM/.

Dylan, B. (1972). The death of Emmett Till. *Broadside ballads, Vol. 6: Broadside reunion*, Warner Bros, Inc. Hollywood, CA.

Federal Bureau of Investigation Report. *Famous cases and criminals*. Retrieved from https://www.fbi.gov/history/famous-cases/emmett-till.

Harris, E. L. (2010). My name is Emmett Till. *Hard Bargain* (album) Laughing House Studios, Nashville, TN, directed by Jack Spence.

Hitchcock, S. (2016). *Ruby Lee and me*. New York: Scholastic.

Huie, W. B. (1956). The shocking story of approved killing in Mississippi. *Look, 20*, 46–50.

Hurst, B., & Pearman, C. J. (2013). Teach reading? But I'm not a reading teacher! *Critical Questions in Education, 4*(3), 225–234.

Identity Charts (2016). *Facing history and ourselves*. Retrieved from https://www.facinghistory.org/resource-library/teaching-strategies/identity-charts.

Levine, E. S. (2000). *Freedom's children: Young civil rights activists tell their own stories*. New York: Puffin Books.

McLaughlin, M. (2012). Reading comprehension: What every teacher needs to know. *The Reading Teacher, 65*(7), 432–440.

Nelson, M. (2005). *A wreath for Emmett Till*. Boston, MA: Houghton Mifflin.

Nitzskin, K., Katzir, T., & Sulkind, S. (2014). Improving reading comprehension one word at a time. *Middle School Journal, 45*(3), 26–32.

PBS. (2017). *Mississippi then, Mississippi now*. Retrieved from www.pbs.org/wgbh/amex/till/sfeature/sf_seg_pop_ms03.html.

PBS. (2017). *People and events: Citizen's councils*. Retrieved from www.pbs.org/wgbh/amex/till/peopleevents/e_councils.html.

PBS. (2017). *People and events: Lynching in America*. Retrieve from http://www.pbs.org/wgbh/amex/till/peopleevents/e_lynch.html.

PBS. (2017). *Primary sources: Reactions in writing*. Retrieved from http://www.pbs.org/wgbh/amex/till/filmmore/ps_reactions.html.

PBS. (2017). *The rise and fall of Jim Crow intergenerational discussion guide.* Retrieved from https://www-tc.pbs.org/wnet/jimcrow/jimcrowguide.pdf.

PBS. (2017). *Sex and race.* Retrieved from www.pbs.org/wgbh/amex/till/sfeature/ sf_relations_01.html.

PBS. (2017). *The shocking story of approved killing in Mississippi.* Retrieved from http://www.pbs.org/wgbh/amex/till/sfeature/sf_look_confession.html.

PBS. (2017). *Teens and segregation.* Retrieved from www.pbs.org/wgbh/amex/till/ sfeature/sf_segregation.html.

Taylor, M. D. (2016). *The road to Memphis.* New York: Puffin Books.

Time (2016). *When one mother defied America: The photo that changed the Civil Rights Movement.* Retrieved from http://time.com/4399793/emmett-till-civil-rights-photo graphy/?xid=fbshare.

Tovani, C. (2000). *I read it, but I don't get it: Comprehension strategies for adolescent readers.* Portland, ME: Stenhouse Publishers.

Chapter 9

Race, Racism, and Power Structures: Reading *All American Boys* in a Social Studies Current Events Course

Shelly Shaffer and A. Suzie Henning

Through an examination of culture, civic ideals, and power, the reading of *All American Boys* provides opportunities for students to engage in analysis and evaluation of current issues. Applying collaborative and cooperative learning strategies that build on students' funds of knowledge (Moll, Amanti, Neff, & Gonzalez, 1992), and drawing on constructivist principles of meaning making through observation and conversation (Farris, 2015), the instructional approaches we offer in this chapter are intended to broadens students' development as citizens in a pluralistic democracy.

Because chapters in *All American Boys* alternate between two perspectives, Rashad's and Quinn's, the study of this novel is strongly aligned to standards that call for students to evaluate authors' differing points of view on the same event and the use of textual evidence to support that evaluation. As students work through the novel, they will understand change and the cultural impact of power, authority, and governance.

ALL AMERICAN BOYS BY JASON REYNOLDS AND BRENDAN KIELY (320 PP.)

All American Boys address the timely issues of police brutality, racism, and advocacy. Rashad, an ROTC cadet and talented artist, is savagely beaten on the sidewalk outside a convenience store after a white police officer accuses him of stealing and assaulting a white woman. Quinn witnesses the beating, and at first decides to ignore what happened. As the word spreads around school, Quinn begins to feel as though he has a responsibility to speak up about what he witnessed, even though others—including teachers—feel it is best not discussed. He and his high school peers and community come together to participate in a peaceful protest to demonstrate their unwillingness to accept what transpired.

BEFORE READING *ALL AMERICAN BOYS*

Activating students' prior knowledge focuses their reading and helps students to make connections before tackling a text (Gallagher, 2004). *All American Boys* is not only relevant to events transpiring today, but the text also situates itself within the historical context of civil rights and equity. In addition, all four dimensions of the C3 Framework for Social Studies (NCSS, 2013) are addressed through analysis of past and current events involving police. Specifically, the novel provides students with opportunities to develop and communicate reflective and nuanced conclusions that can lead to informed action.

Exploring the Historical Context of Civil Rights and Equity

As students prepare to examine, analyze, and discuss the issues of race and racism in this novel, having students compare and contrast police activity during the Civil Rights Movement in Little Rock, Birmingham, and Montgomery to contemporary events in Ferguson, Minneapolis, and New York is a great start. Guiding students through the past and into the present as a way to explore these issues, students can begin to consider how people and organizations promote unity and diversity with concepts such as *fairness*, *equity*, and *justice*. The inclusion of current primary sources surrounding police brutality in the United States can also aide students in seeing the relevance of these concepts today.

Given the sensitivity of race and racism in both the text and our current society, teachers should assist learners in articulating personal perspectives in responsible ways. It is important that teachers facilitate discussion of these difficult topics in their efforts to move students through their examination of how perceptions, attitudes, values, and beliefs impact not only the development of personal identity, but the impact of these personal beliefs on others. Some guiding questions teachers can pose to lead discussions are the following:

- What does it mean to "protect and serve?"
- How has the role of the protester and police changed during periods of unrest and war?
- How does status as an insider/outsider within a community change the interpretation of events in moments of crisis?

- What is the obligation of participatory citizens in a multicultural, democratic society when American voices are silenced?

Developing responses to these questions encourages students to interact with important social studies themes by thinking critically about culture, power, and authority over time; people and their environment; and identity as a civic actor (Adler et al., 2010).

Getting Students Excited to Read

Getting adolescents excited to read can be an obstacle for many educators, let alone social studies teachers who are introducing young adult (YA) literature into a content that does not typically utilize this text form. Book talking is one way to get students interested. During a book talk on *All American Boys*, an overview of the historical connections is the recommended first step. Following guidelines of researchers and practitioners, the instructor have students examine and analyze the cover of the book (Atwell, 2014; Bond, 2011; Kittle, 2012; Lesesne, 2003). Teachers then pose questions about the cover to get students thinking about the concepts they will encounter in their reading and guide them in making connections to the historical events examined. For instance, the cover image depicts a young man with his hands in the air with red and blue lights in the background. In an effort to activate students' prior knowledge, ask them to make inferences based on the cover image. Questions teachers may pose: What do you think book is about based on the cover? What might the cover artist be indicating by portraying a person with their hands up on the book cover image? What current events can you think of that relate to this image?

Previewing a passage from a text prior to its reading is said to also motivate students and activate prior knowledge (Bond, 2011; Buehl, 2014; Burke, 2013; Gallagher, 2004; Kittle, 2012). We suggest that teachers share the passage that begins with ' "Ma'am are you okay?' the officer asked, concerned" (p. 20) and ends with "I let out a wail, a sound that came from somewhere deep inside. One I had never made before, coming from a feeling I had never felt before" (p. 22). This scene is the stimulus that drives the plot.

After exploring historical connections, previewing the cover, and listening to a scene, students should make predictions about the novel. Schmitt (1990) purports, "Predicting the content of a story promotes active comprehension by giving readers a purpose for reading (i.e., to verify the predictions). Evaluating predictions and generating new ones as necessary enhances the constructive nature of the reading process" (p. 455). These predictions can be shared in several ways. One way is through a think-pair-share activity. While this activity can be seen as simplistic, we recommend that students employ a higher-order thinking version of this strategy, drawing on textual evidence from the scene read to support prediction. In collaborative teams, students are asked to combine their predictions and present them to the class. The teacher tracks each group's predictions, making them visible by writing them on a whiteboard or large piece of paper. Thus, as students read, opportunities to revisit and reassess their predictions are present.

Because failure to understand even a few words can hinder students' comprehension, key academic vocabulary should be highlighted prior to reading any text. One way to approach this is through the inclusion of a Vocabulary Rating Scale (VRS). Vacca and Vacca (1999) suggest that the use of this strategy not only gets readers to analyze what they know about a topic through rating their own knowledge, but the teacher can get an idea of the knowledge the student and the class bring to the reading. Using a VRS graphic organizer, each student individually rates their familiarity with the terms presented. If students indicate that they are familiar with the definition, they must provide one as evidence. If they indicate that they have heard the word before, but are unsure of what it means, or if they indicate they have no idea what a word means, they must make a prediction, drawing on what has been discussed and examined thus far. Some suggested terms are *unity, diversity, justice, equity, fairness, rights,* and *responsibility.* Once completed individually, place students into groups and have them share their familiarity and understanding of the terms with each other. Once all group members have shared, they develop definitions for key terms as a team to share with the whole class. Discuss the similarities and differences that are noted with your class. From this, stems the creation of a shared definition for class use.

Other important social studies concepts central to understanding the novel include *culture, power, authority, social justice,* and *civic actor.* Just like vocabulary, these concepts should also be explored and defined prior to reading. One way to approach this is through the analysis of song lyrics. Some songs that lend themselves to the exploration of these concepts include "How Come, How Long" (Edmonds & Wonder, 1996) or "Concrete Angel" (Crosby & Bentley, 2001). Citing evidence from the lyrics, students consider the role of individuals in society when confronted with injustice, and the responsibility to others when one observes misconduct or harmful behavior done to another person.

WHILE READING *ALL AMERICAN BOYS*

After activating and building students' background knowledge and providing a platform from which to draw historical connections, there are a number of strategies teachers could employ as students read. Because we are asking students to take risks in sharing their personal perspectives and beliefs about issues that can be deemed sensitive (*race, culture,* and *power*), the use of technology while reading offers students safe spaces to share and explore.

The use of a discussion board is an effective tool for aiding comprehension and in deepening students' thinking about a book (Bender, 2012). Through this strategy, students individually respond to questions posed by the teacher. Their responses should draw on personal beliefs, understandings of historical content studied, and *All American Boys*. As a means to promote dialogue, students should be required to respond to peers' posts.

All American Boys is divided into sections based on the one-week time-frame that passes between the beating and the final march. The following are suggested discussion board questions for different sections of the novel:

- "Friday" (pp. 5–40): Compare and contrast Quinn and Rashad. Which character do you most relate to and why?
- "Saturday" and "Sunday" (pp. 43–120): Analyze the different reactions of Quinn's and Rashad's family and friends to Rashad's beating. Why might people be reacting so differently? How would you react if you were in Quinn's shoes?
- "Monday" through "Thursday" (pp. 123–282): Why do you think that many of the teachers at school are ignoring the situation? What should teachers and/or the school have done?
- "Friday" (pp. 285–310): In what ways was this situation resolved? Why did Quinn decide to go? Why did Rashad decide to go? What would you have done?

Discussion post criteria should measure students' comprehension of the text and connections to the content, critical reading (Blake, 1998; Lewison, Flint, & Van Sluys, 2002; Martin, Smolen, Oswald, & Milam, 2012; McDonald, 2004; Rosenblatt, 1994, 1995), and the use of textual evidence to support content and personal connections. These criteria encourage students to engage in the online discussion in an authentic way.

Another technology application that could be used to foster discussion of the text is blogging. Huffaker (2004) suggests that blogging can help students in both self-reflection and self-evaluation. Because blogs are public, the process of blogging requires students to become more critical in their writing (Williams & Jacobs, 2004). Students can create a blog page that records their interactions with *All American Boys*. The blog should include visuals, music, and other multimedia that offer insight into the blogger's text-to-self and text-to-content connections. Teachers can direct students to read and comment on their classmates' blogs via the comment link.

This task can be approached in two ways: informally or formally. Informally, students respond without teacher prompting. Through this approach, students share their interactions from a personal perspective. These responses become a starting point for student-led discussions. In a formal approach students are prompted to respond to teacher created questions, simulating a teacher-led discussion. No matter the approach, blogging as a tool for discussing the text offers students an opportunity to develop skills in writing and analysis.

AFTER READING *ALL AMERICAN BOYS*

Social studies standards encourage students to become actors in their world (Adler et al., 2010). Through post-reading activities, students continue connecting themes to historical and contemporary events as a way of developing a stance toward social justice and the duties of citizenship.

Teachers can aide students in the exploration of nonviolent protests of the past such as the Birmingham Bus Boycott, the March on Washington in 1963, and the Student Non-Violent Coordinating Committee, with current protests such as the Black Lives Matter Movement and the Women's March on Washington. Events in *All American Boys* that relate well to this discussion are the nonviolent demonstrations protesting Rashad's beating, Quinn's struggles with the decision to join the protest, and how their communities' responded.

In cooperative learning groups, students can brainstorm ways they could become activists in their school community. This brainstorming may lead to the creation of platforms that contain historical explanations, analysis of the impact of current events that have fueled racial tensions, and a persuasive argument for action. Students may use their platform to either create a public service announcement (PSA) or a "Message in a Bottle" that educates others on the issue. The sharing of their "Message in a Bottle" projects moves students forward, encouraging them to demonstrate civic action. As a means to reach a larger audience, students could publish their PSA in a larger forum, such as on social media websites (Facebook, Instagram), or even in the creation of a wiki.

EXTENSION ACTIVITIES BEYOND *ALL AMERICAN BOYS*

Extension activities provide opportunities for students to connect with *All American Boys* in creative, engaging ways. Extension activities can be differentiated by allowing students to demonstrate evidence of their learning in multiple ways. By offering choices that ask students to think beyond questions of comprehension, teachers can move students toward critical thinking through analysis, evaluation, and synthesis (Bloom, 1956). Below are some activities that teachers may wish to employ:

Song Lyrics

Students can spotlight a theme through the creation of music and then present to the class. Use *Hip-Hop U.S. History* (Harrison & Rappaport, 2006) as a guide for students.

Create a Graphic Novel

Students, either individually or in cooperative groups, can convert *All American Boys* into a graphic novel. Students should determine four-six key events or chapters from the text. Using imagery and dialogue directly from the text, students depict the events in graphic form. Use the *9/11 Commission Report* (National Commission on Terrorists Attacks, 2004) and its corresponding graphic novel (Jacobson & Colón, 2006) as a guide.

Dream Catcher

The characters presented in the book have dreams and life goals that are changed by the events they experience. Students can create a dream catcher that includes symbols of dreams for each character. Dream symbols can be visually displayed on the dream catcher. Use Langston Hughes' poem "Dream Deferred" (1994) to stimulate students' exploration of dreams.

Bookmark

Young adult literature publishers often market texts using bookmarks that visually represent the key ideas of the novel. Students can summarize their understanding of key ideas by creating a bookmark to market *All American Boys*.

CONCLUSION

Through the reading of *All American Boys*, students explore social studies content in a unique, authentic, and constructivist way while simultaneously practicing literacy skills in reading, writing, listening, and speaking. Including this novel in a social studies unit may motivate students to interact with the social studies themes of *identity*, *power*, *governance*, and *culture* in a way that cannot be achieved through traditional instruction. Not only does this novel address important current issues by evoking history beyond memorizing names and dates, it also urges students to examine their beliefs and attitudes and take action.

Annotated List of Related YA Literature

The Absolutely True Diary of a Part-Time Indian by Sherman Alexie and Ellen Forney (229 pp.)

This modern classic is the story of Junior, a Native American who is growing up in Washington State. Junior decides to go to school off the reservation; and as a result, he faces ostracism by both his white classmates and his home community. Readers realize that Junior's identity is connected to his sense of belonging.

We Were Here by Matt de la Peña (368 pp.)

Miguel is sentenced to live in a group home for one year, and the book is a series of journal entries Miguel is required to write as part of his sentence. When Miguel and two other boys try to escape their confinement and go on the run, they become humanized and readers empathize with the characters as their personal experiences and struggles are revealed.

How It Went Down by Kekla Magoon (336 pp.)

Tariq, a sixteen-year-old African American male, is shot on the street by a white man. The story, as told by bystanders, witnesses, and others, addresses the complexity of the issue of shootings and violence. This novel examines current events from multiples perspectives.

Yaqui Delgado Wants to Kick Your Ass by Meg Medina (272 pp.)

Piddy Sanchez is the target of bullying because Yaqui Delgado, a gang member, thinks she "isn't Latin enough." Piddy tries to avoid Yaqui, but she eventually has to decide who she is instead of trying to hide in fear. This novel examines cultural identity and the question of what it means to be part of a certain culture.

REFERENCES

Adler, S. A., Altoff, P., Marri, A. R., McFarland, M. A., McGrew, C., Sorenson, M. E., Thornton, S. J., Tyson, C. A., Warren, Z., & Wendt, B. (2010). *National curriculum standards for social studies: A framework for teaching, learning, and assessment.* Silver Spring, MD: National Council for the Social Studies.

Alexie, S., & Forney, E. (2009). *The absolutely true diary of a part-time Indian.* New York: Little Brown.

Atwell, N. (2014). *In the middle, third edition: A lifetime of learning about writing, reading, and adolescents* (3rd ed.). Portsmouth, NH: Heinemann.

Bender, T. (2012). *Discussion-based online teaching to enhance student learning: Theory, practice, and assessment* (2nd ed.). Sterling, VA: Stylus.

Blake, B. E. (1998). Critical reader response in an urban classroom: Creating cultural texts to engage diverse readers. *Theory into Practice, 37*(3), 238–243.

Bloom, B. (1984). *Taxonomy of educational objectives book 1: Cognitive domain,* 2nd ed. Boston, MA: Addison Wesley.

Bond, E. (2011). *Literature and the young adult reader.* Boston, MA: Pearson.

Buehl, D. (2014). *Classroom strategies for interactive learning* (4th ed.). Newark, DE: International Reading Association.

Burke, J. (2013). *The English teacher's companion: A completely new guide to classroom, curriculum, and the profession* (4th ed.). Portsmouth, NH: Heinemann.

Crosby, R., & Bentley, S. (2001). Concrete angel (Recorded by McBride, M.). On *Greatest Hits* (CD). New York: Sony Legacy.

De la Peña, M. (2009). *We were here.* New York: Delacorte Press.

Edmonds, K., & Wonder, S. (1996). How come, how long. On *The day* (CD). New York: Epic Records.

Farris, P. (2015) *Elementary and middle school social studies: An interdisciplinary, multicultural approach* (7th ed.). Long Grove, IL: Waveland.

Gallagher, K. (2004). *Deeper reading.* Portland, ME: Stenhouse.

Harrison, B., & Rappaport, A. (2006). *Hip-Hop U.S. history: The new and innovative approach to learning American history (Flocabulary study guides).* Kennebunkport, ME: Cider Mill Press.

Huffaker, D. (2004). The educated blogger: Using weblogs to promote literacy in the Classroom. *AACE Journal, 13*(2), 91–98.

Hughes, L. (1994). Dream deferred. *The collected poems of Langston Hughes.* New York: Alfred Knopf, Inc.

Jacobson, S., & Colón, E. (2006). *The 9/11 report: A graphic adaptation.* New York: Hill and Wang.

Kittle, P. (2012). *Book love: Developing depth, stamina, and passion in adolescent readers.* Portsmouth, NH: Heinemann.

Lesesne, T. (2003). *Making the match: The right book for the right reader at the right time, grades 4–12.* Portland, ME: Stenhouse.

Lewison, M., Flint, A. S., & Van Sluys, K. (2002). Taking on critical literacy: The journey of newcomers and novices. *Language Arts, 79*(5), 382–392.

Magoon, K. (2015). *How it went down.* New York: Henry Holt and Company, LLC.

Martin, L. A., Smolen, L. A., Oswald, R. A., & Milam, J. L. (2012). Preparing students for global citizenship in the twenty-first century: Integrating social justice through global literature. *Social Studies, 103*(4), 158–164.

McDonald, L. (2004). Moving from reader response to critical reading: Developing 10–11-year-olds' ability as analytical readers of literary texts. *Literacy, 38*(1), 17–23.

Medina, M. (2014). *Yaqui Delgado wants to kick your ass.* Somerville, MA: Candlewick.

Moll, L. C., Amanti, C., Neff, D., & Gonzalez, N. (1992). Funds of knowledge for teaching: Using a qualitative approach to connect homes and classrooms. *Theory into Practice, 31*(2), 132–141.

National Commission on Terrorist Attacks upon the United States (2004). *The 9/11 commission report: Final report of the National Commission on Terrorist Attacks upon the United States.* Washington, DC: National Commission on Terrorist Attacks upon the United States.

National Council for the Social Studies (NCSS) (2013). *The college, career, and civic life (c3) framework for social studies state standards: Guidance for enhancing the rigor of k-12 civics, economics, geography, and history.* Silver Spring, MD: NCSS.

Reynolds, J., & Kiely, B. (2015). *All American boys.* New York: Atheneum.

Rosenblatt, L. (1994). *The reader, the text, the poem: The transactional theory of the literary work.* Carbondale, IL: Southern Illinois University Press.

Rosenblatt, L. (1995). *Literature as exploration* (5th ed.). New York: The Modern Language Association of America.

Schmitt, M. C. (1990). A questionnaire to measure children's awareness of strategic reading processes. *The Reading Teacher, 43*(7), 454–461.

Vacca, R. T., & Vacca J. L. (1999). *Content area reading: Literacy and learning across the curriculum* (6th ed.). Boston, MA: Addison-Wesley Educational.

Williams, J. B., & Jacobs, J. (2004). Exploring the use of blogs as learning spaces in the higher education sector. *Australasian Journal of Educational Technology, 20*(2), 232–237.

Chapter 10

The Eyes of van Gogh: Searching for Identity and Expression through Art

Robert Jordan and Mike DiCicco

The Eyes of van Gogh is a story about a high school student who uses art to escape the hardships of her life and adolescence. The story touches on relatable themes for young adults including fitting in, adjusting to a new school, and finding an identity. It also touches on deeper themes of depression and family. Jude is inspired by Vincent van Gogh, and as such, van Gogh's life and art are a prominent part of the story as it serves as motivation and an escape for Jude. Jude sees van Gogh's motivations for suicide similar to her own struggles as she discovers how art allows her to deal with the hardships in her own life. The novel is an excellent example of how art and personal expression can play a crucial role in how adolescents learn, see the world, and as a way to navigate adolescence.

THE EYES OF VAN GOGH BY CATHRYN CLINTON (216 PP.)

Jude has spent her seventeen years moving from one town to the next as her single, alcoholic mother goes from one failed relationship to another. When the two relocate to be near Jude's ailing grandmother, Jude holds out hope that she can finally find a stable life. When she develops friendships with two classmates and gains the attention of a shy and studious football star, Jude believes her solitary existence can finally be replaced by happiness. Unfortunately, as her relationship with her boyfriend sours and her grandmother's health fails, Jude discovers that her deep connection to Vincent van Gogh's art extends to his tortured life and thoughts of suicide. This novel vividly demonstrates how art can help an individual make connections and express feelings in profound ways, especially for those who have no other voice.

CONNECTING ART AND LITERACY

Clinton weaves in elements of design, composition, and art history into the narrative, making it a solid literary complement to visual art instruction. *The Eyes of van Gogh* can be used to introduce art history, as well as prompt discussions on composition, use of color, symbolism, and emotion. Importantly, the novel can be used to address a number of standards that addresses how artists and designers shape artistic investigations and how people create art, spaces, and designs that shape and empower their lives. The activities provided in this chapter offer teachers an opportunity to address the Visual Arts Model Corner Assessment where, "Students use knowledge gained to experiment, plan, and make their own artworks to express meaning relevant to a theme or idea important to the group" (NCAS, 2014). In addition, Jude's dedication, discipline, and willingness to experiment, fail, and persevere are all attributes emerging artists should emulate, offering inspiration in this character.

Visual Art and Literacy Connections

There is a commonality between visual art and writing. Both are composition processes; the artist and writer equally seek to convey meaning through their medium. When both are integrated into the classroom, these commonalities enhance each other in a cyclical manner in ways they cannot on their own.

Both painters and writers use light and color for compositional purposes, setting the tone and mood for their work. The symbolic use of color (i.e., red for passion and gray for mystery) adds additional layers of meaning just as effectively in both visual art and literature. Authors and artists manipulate the impact and emotions of their works through object placement, movement, rhythm, unity, and balance of their settings and characters. The sense of poetry in visual art and writing is enhanced by the composer's choice of color, body language, and scenic elements. When all these components are skillfully used, the artist/author lifts the veil between the viewer/reader, making him or her feel as if they have entered the reality of the work.

As an extension, when students can both view and read works that contain these creative elements, they in turn learn to incorporate them into their own visual and text-based compositions. Students who are exposed to great works of art and literature, and skillfully guided by a teacher who reveals connections, are able to create pieces that contain multiple layers of meaning and recognize more than surface details when viewing the works of others.

BEFORE READING *THE EYES OF VAN GOGH*

Who Is van Gogh?

Clinton's novel blends art history, art, and adolescence in a story about belonging, mental health, and finding ways to express ourselves. To build students' schema before reading the novel, students should examine van Gogh's life and work. Understanding van Gogh's life will help students understand Jude's point of view and actions. In particular, van Gogh's struggle with depression and his suicide play a pertinent role in this novel. Having students discover biographical information about van Gogh through Webquests or other research projects will help them gain the background needed to understand the connection between van Gogh and Jude in the novel. Primary sources such as van Gogh's letters (1996) will give students a glimpse into his mind through his own writing. The letters are enlightening, moving, and haunting.

In addition to learning about his life, students should become familiar with his work and style. While there are many books and websites that highlight van Gogh's art, we suggest using Google's Art Project, a free online database of art from all major museums. Teachers and students can explore and read about van Gogh's work, examine ultra-high quality images of his art, where examining brush strokes and colors is as easy as zooming in. Students learning about his work and post-impressionism help contextualize Clinton's novel and helps the reader further understand Jude's feelings and motivations.

The style and composition of van Gogh's art and other post-impressionists can lead to a discussion about how art is used to express mood and feeling. In particular, the study of "Starry Night" would be fitting for this novel as it is referenced often and becomes a plot point in the text. While many students will have some familiarity with painting and drawing techniques from either formal classes or work on their own, they will benefit from exposure to the techniques and artists Clinton weaves into the novel. Present a video of van Gogh, post-impressionism, and various visual art mediums to provide the necessary background knowledge to enrich students' understanding of both the novel and art. Bring in books with reproductions of the pieces mentioned throughout the story. In addition, posting examples of van Gogh's paintings, especially ones mentioned in the novel—*Murder of Crows, Bedroom in Arles,* and *The Night Café*—will also give students the experience with the paintings that Jude is afforded in her art class.

Mental Illness and Art

Within this novel, Jude's connection with van Gogh extends beyond his art and into his struggles with depression and thoughts of suicide. Consequently, it may be beneficial to have a discussion about mental illness and art. According to the Center for Disease Control (CDC) (2015), 17 percent of students seriously considered attempting suicide in 2014, and suicide is the third leading cause of death for teens. Research highlights the benefits of using texts in the classroom for students learning text-to-self connections (Glasgow, 2011) where literature response is a transaction between the reader and the text (Rosenblatt, 1996), and readers make connections when they see themselves in fictional characters (Wilhelm & Smith, 1996). A component of teen suicide prevention is sharing books on the topic and having discussions with students (Fisher, 2005). Novels that thoughtfully address these topics, even for students who are not struggling with depression or suicidal thoughts, allow students to develop empathy as they come to see how these feelings may affect them and their classmates (Rybakova, Piotrowski, & Harper, 2013).

During the course of *The Eyes of van Gogh*, Jude experiences increasing feelings of isolation and depression. When she says to herself, "Maybe it would be better if you weren't here" (p. 186), she begins planning on taking her own life. Only when she makes the connection between her painting and her desire to find her place in the world does she realize, she is not alone and changes her mind. Exposing students to these common feelings can also help them to see they are not alone, and there are better ways to cope with self-destructive emotions. A discussion about what depression is and how it can be treated can be helpful, and a discussion about the benefits of art therapy on depression would be especially poignant for Clinton's novel. The pre-reading questions below should spark discussions on the nature of art, preconceptions about artists, and the role of art in society.

- Who makes a living from art?
- In what ways are mental illness and creativity linked? (p.12)
- Explain the difference between depth and perspective. (p. 86)
- In what ways did Post-Impressionists express mood and feeling?
- What is depression? Discuss some ways depression can be treated?
- What are the benefits of art therapy on depression?

READING *THE EYES OF VAN GOGH*

After exploring van Gogh's life and work, post-impressionism, and mental health, students are ready to read. The first person narrative helps give the reader an inside look at how Jude thinks and processes the world around her. We see her struggle and find solace in art. As students read the text, they should focus on the narrator, especially noting the hints showing how she is feeling, attempting to deceive friends and family about how she feels, and her intended actions. Jude provides valuable insights into how an adolescent who is depressed may interact with others and why. Strategies that help focus on the narrator such as a double-entry journal (Beers, 2003) or character sketches (Wilhelm, 2004) can help students keep track of what Jude is thinking and why she behaves in certain ways. As students track Jude's development, comparing similarities between Jude and van Gogh (eyes, tragic love life, thoughts of suicide) through the use of a T-chart in a reading journal (Beers, 2003), students can "see" their connections.

Setting is a critical component of Clinton's novel. Each setting presented within the novel helps to highlight Jude's thoughts, feelings, and emotions. Jude's friend Jazz has a home Jude describes as warm, comfortable, and safe—the way a house should be. By contrast, Jude's home is described as a cold, desolate, and barren place where she is forced to go every night. Further, the railroad tracks provide a setting where Jude can escape and be herself, but it also doubles as a place where she is isolated. The train itself represents a way to escape, as it is literally a form of travel, but Jude sees the train as a possible different form of escape. Finally, art class is Jude's refuge in school, and Clinton offers a description of a warm and supportive classroom environment. It is the one place where Jude can be her real self and is valued. Having students examine the many settings while they read, can aid them in their understanding of the story while simultaneously exploring Jude's feelings and motivations.

Clinton's use of vivid language to describe each setting and the impact it has on Jude's actions, allows students opportunities to incorporate art into their reading. Having students create visuals (perhaps as part of their double-entry diary), or implementing strategies such as Sketch to Stretch (Harste, 2014) to highlight these connections could help students visualize, comprehend, and engage in the story. Another approach to emphasizing the connections could be through a Visual Reader Response Diary. As students read the novel, they note their thoughts and feelings about the characters, setting, action, mood, and so on through sketches. Their drawings should not just be literal depictions of the story's events, but rather interpretations of the emotions evoked by the characters' thoughts and actions. To extend this, students could create multiple images using van Gogh's style.

AFTER READING *THE EYES OF VAN GOGH*

Writing about and Discussing What We Read

Meaningful discussions can occur after students finish reading the novel and we recommend these as discussion prompts:

- What is concentrated and mystical about "Starry Night"? (p. 11)
- Describe the evolution of van Gogh's early drawings to his later paintings. How does this parallel Jude's progression as an artist? (p. 23)

- Chart characteristics and actions—eyes, tragic love life, suicidal thoughts, and so on—that Jude and van Gogh have in common.
- What is reality and how do molecules portray the concept? (p. 87)
- How does "showing things differently, even incorrectly" reveal deeper truths about them? (p. 90)
- How can art "keep you from feeling truly alone"? (p. 107)
- After her grandmother's death, why does Jude paint her mother with the body of a girl? (p. 172)
- There are several times in the book that the author uses boldface type. Why does Clinton use this technique? Who is speaking? (pp. 148, 186)
- Describe the evolution of van Gogh's early drawings to his later paintings. How does this parallel Jude's progression as an artist?

Extension Activities beyond The Eyes of van Gogh

The Eyes of van Gogh lends itself to a plethora of opportunities for students to learn beyond the text. Some extension activities that students can perform are provided below:

Biography and Art

Write a short biography of an artist of your choice with accompanying art works that reflect themes and/or style of that artist that are meaningful to you. The drawings should be original creations (not reproductions of the studied artist) and demonstrate your interpretation of the artist's vision, settings in your life inspired by the artist's experiences, or portraits of people you know influenced by the artist's style.

Quotes and Art

Using interviews, biographies, and articles about an artist of your choice select three quotes from that artist that speak to you or are particularly meaningful. Create illustrations, such as drawings, paintings, and/or photographs, that best represent the artist's sentiments.

Composition and Juxtaposition

On p. 24 Jude states that you need the unexpected as an element of composition. This is often achieved by introducing an element in juxtaposition to the theme or content of the work. Create a composition that contains an unexpected element, keeping in mind that the choice of the unexpected should add a layer of meaning to the composition.

Symbols, Color, and Art

Clinton points out the importance of color and its symbolic meanings (see pp. 61, 143, 158, 162). Create drawings or paintings in which color plays a vital and meaningful role. These drawings can be inspired by settings or characters in the novel, but the selection of color should be carefully considered to represent the desired emotion. Be prepared to explain your choice of colors and what they mean to you.

CONCLUSION

Cathryn Clinton's deft weaving of art, art history, teen identity, and frank depiction of depression make *The Eyes of van Gogh* an excellent choice for readers to feel the power of art and self-expression. By helping students realize their vision through art and literature, teachers can help them to find creative outlets to help them traverse life's problems through productive solutions. While the strategies and activities presented in this chapter focus on what students can do with the text as they develop art knowledge and literacy skills, this novel also houses an opportunity for teachers to learn about constructive criticism. Jude remarks that Ms. Dennis displays honest criticism of her students' art work (pp. 85–86). While there may not be a "right way" to create a piece, you should always want to do more. Teachers can use this approach in critiquing students' work, keeping in mind that one's words should never squelch a student's desire to create more.

Annotated List of Related YA Literature

Graffiti Moon by Cath Crowley (264 pp.)

Lucy is in love with Shadow, a mysterious graffiti artist whose legend may not live up to reality. Ed and Lucy share a love/hate relationship, and Dylan loves Daisy but doesn't know how to tell her. Throw into the mix a gang of thugs set on revenge. *Graffiti Moon* takes readers on a whirlwind twenty-four hours of a group of young adults in search of love, identity, and discovering what is really important.

Da Vinci's Tiger by L. M. Elliott (287 pp.)

Ginevra de' Benci wants to share her poetry in Renaissance Florence, but her social status makes it difficult until Bernardo Bembo, a Venetian ambassador, comes along and introduces Ginerva to a host of artists and philosophers. Chosen to be his platonic muse, Bernado commissions Leonardo da Vinci to paint her portrait. Through da Vinci's painting, she comes to discover her voice and artistic talents.

The Vigilante Poets of Selwyn Academy by Kate Hattemer (336 pp.)

When a trashy reality television show takes over Selwyn Arts Academy, Ethan and his multitalented best friends use poetry to fight back. They create an underground publication inspired by Ezra Pound to keep their school from being torn apart. Unfortunately, they soon learn that they have enemies in more places than they could have imagined.

The Fine Art of Truth or Dare by Melissa Jensen (400 pp.)

Ella doesn't fit in at exclusive Willing School, but she's happy hanging out with her equally quirky friends Frankie and Sadie. While being a South Philly scholarship student is enough to stop Ella from fitting in at Willing, the fact that she's in love with (and talks to) Edward Willing, a nineteenth-century artist, doesn't help things. When Ella falls in love with the most popular boy in school, will she be able to live up to her fantasy?

Every You, Every Me by David Levithan (245 pp.)

Ariel's suicidal tendencies, dramatic mood swings, and disappearance send Evan into a spiral of confusion and guilt. Evan's anxious thoughts are told through stream-of-consciousness, crossed-out passages revealing his increasing feelings of loneliness and grief. The novel is uniquely presented with mysterious black-and-white photos inserted into the story, engaging the reader into Evan's search for the truth.

Between Shades of Gray by Ruta Sepetys (344 pp.)

Fifteen-year-old Lina is torn from her family in 1941 Lithuania and sent to a brutal work camp in distant Siberia. Through her art Lina discovers her greatest hope, creating drawings that she desperately hopes will find their way to her father. Even as she depicts the horrors of war, Lina's love of life and the kindness of others show the human spirit can thrive in the face of great adversity.

REFERENCES

Beers, K. (2003). *When kids can't read, what teachers can do.* Portsmouth, NH: Heinemann.

Center for Disease Control (2015). *Suicide facts at a glance 2015.* Retrieved from www.cdc.gov/violenceprevention/pdf/suicide-datasheet-a.pdf.

Clinton, C. (2007). *The eyes of van Gogh*. Somerville, MA: Candlewick.

Crowley, C. (2012). *Graffiti moon*. New York: Knopf.

Elliott, L. M. (2015). *Da Vinci's tiger*. New York: Katherine Tegen Books.

Fisher, D. (2005). The literacy educator's role in suicide prevention. *Journal of Adolescent & Adult Literacy, 48*(5), 364–373.

Glasgow, J. (2001). Teaching social justice through young adult literature. *English Journal, 90*(6), 54–61.

Harste, J. C. (2014). The art of learning to be critically literate1. *Language Arts, 92*(2), 90–102.

Hattemer, K. (2014). *The vigilante poets of Selwyn academy*. New York: Knopf.

Jensen, M. (2012). *The fine art of truth or dare*. London, UK: Penguin Group.

Levithan, D. (2011). *Every you, every me*. New York: Alfred A. Knopf.

National Core Art Standards (2014). *Dance, media arts, music, theatre and visual arts*. Retrieved from http://www.nationalartsstandards.org.

Rosenblatt, L. (1996). *Literature as exploration* (5th ed.). New York: Modern Language Association of America.

Rybakova, K., Piotrowski, A., & Harper, E. (2013). Teaching controversial young adult literature with the common core. *Wisconsin English Journal, 55*(1), 37–45.

Sepetys, R. (2011). *Between shades of gray*. New York: Penguin.

van Gogh, V. (1996). *The letters of Vincent van Gogh*. London, UK: Penguin Classics.

Wilhelm, J. D. (2004). *Reading is seeing*. New York: Scholastic.

Wilhelm, J. D., & Smith, M. W. (1996). *You gotta be the book: Teaching engaged and reflective reading with adolescents*. New York: Teachers College Press.

Chapter 11

Understanding Theater in *Drama High: The Incredible True Story of a Brilliant Teacher, a Struggling Town, and the Magic of Theater*

Jeffrey S. Kaplan and Elizabeth Brendel Horn

Drama High: The Incredible True Story of a Brilliant Teacher, a Struggling Town, and the Magic of Theater is a fascinating, discerning, and engaging read for understanding the theatrical arts while simultaneously providing a rich and complex portrait of one high school drama's teacher journey to bridge the world of drama with the drama of adolescence. This rich and complex narrative chronicles how one high school drama teacher changed the lives of countless adolescents as he transformed an ordinary high school drama program into a world class theater program that changed the lives of its teen participants both off and on the stage.

Seeing themselves in the characters presented in this nonfiction text will encourage students to deeply invest in the literary and theatrical exercises presented, thus strengthening their own skills. Simultaneously, accompanying the text with a theatrical exploration of the themes, emotions, and characters within it, will help students develop empathy for others and learn how to more honestly express emotions. The constant interplay between expressing oneself through writing and expressing oneself orally will enable students to build upon a diverse set of academic and life skills.

DRAMA HIGH: THE INCREDIBLE TRUE STORY OF A BRILLIANT TEACHER, A STRUGGLING TOWN, AND THE MAGIC OF THEATER BY MICHAEL SOKOLOVE (338 PP.)

Drama High opens with Cameron Mackintosh, the esteemed, highly acclaimed Broadway and International producer (*Cats, Phantom of the Opera, Miss Saigon*) arriving at Harry S. Truman High in Levittown, Pennsylvania. In his chauffeured driven stretch limousine with entourage in tow,

121

Mackintosh has journeyed from Manhattan to watch a high school performance of *Les Miserables* because word had spread that the production was
"that good." He had heard from others in the theatrical community—that Lou
Volpe, the high school drama teacher, was responsible for wonderful productions that far exceeded normal high school fare. And he had to see it himself.

This revealing and detailed nonfiction narrative spotlights one high school
year (2011–2012) in Volpe's drama program. Volpe and his students produce
and perform the play *Good Boys and True* and the musical *Spring Awakening*, both of which address issues of sex, violence, sexuality, and coming of
age. In telling detail and unapologetic language, Sokolove reveals how Volpe
pushed his student actors, treating them like working professionals; and how,
as a result of this rigorous training, they were inspired and changed forever.
Within this theater ensemble students experience growth academically, per-
sonally, and ultimately, professionally. Sokolove chronicles these changes
through the intimate details of the lives of Volpe's current and former students. Their individual journeys combine into a collective narrative of the
transformative potential of the high school theater experience.

As the narrator describes his dedicated teacher and his significant impact
on the lives of the high school community and other high school drama
programs throughout the United States, we learn many things: how a well-
developed and impassioned high school theater arts program can teach its
participants about acting, writing, performing, creating, building, cooperat-
ing, organizing, and living life; the value of improvisation and the demands
of memorization; the gratitude found in teamwork and the strength derived
from strong individuality; the limitless possibilities of high school drama
productions; and the incredible opportunities for theater to discuss and reveal
issues of social justice.

CONNECTING THEATER AND LITERACY

There are many correlations and opportunities for connecting national
standards—specifically the National Council Teachers of English (NCTE)
and International Reading Association (IRA) Standards for English language
arts (ELA)—through theater lessons, activities, and discussion starters, which
can be used to enhance adolescents' understanding of both the theater arts
and social justice issues. We explore how Sokolove's memoir can be used to
enhance and reinforce students' engagement with text, with theater, and with
understanding the human condition.

Drama High's narrator examines how the topical subject matters approached
by Volpe with his high school students in their theater productions draw parallels to their own everyday problems and concerns. Through their theater

program, students develop the emotional maturity to better understand both the plays that they are producing and their personal lives through their parallels. Meanwhile, the repetition, analysis, imagination, and emotional investment required to interpret a theatrical text allow students to develop their written, reading, and verbal literary skills. Their investment in and passion for this art form allows these learning gains to emerge authentically through the theater-making process.

In this chapter, we have included before-, during-, and after-reading activities that emphasize the use of creative drama exercises to enhance instruction. We have also included a list of open-ended discussion questions for use with this book. Designed to encourage both personal reflection and interpersonal dialogue, these activities cater to a wide variety of learners and abilities and are accessible to all regardless of formal theater training. In addition, these activities span a breadth of theater skills: performance as well as playwriting, directing, and design, further allowing students to express themselves theatrically on multiple planes to cater to their interests and expand their understanding of and appreciation for theater art. These suggested activities, to be used in conjunction with the class reading of *Drama High*, are also widely applicable to the study of other fiction and nonfiction sources.

BEFORE READING *DRAMA HIGH: THE INCREDIBLE TRUE STORY OF A BRILLIANT TEACHER, A STRUGGLING TOWN, AND THE MAGIC OF THEATER*

Adolescents can read *Drama High* from cover to cover, or in spurts. Chapters and passages can stand on their own as they tell separate stories about unique characters, events, and plays that were produced by this daring high school drama teacher. As remarked, the language used by teachers and students at times can be frank and visceral, and teachers are encouraged to read this work before they share it with their students. With that said, teachers will find plenty in this book that their students will find wholly relatable and consequential to their immediate lives.

Ask Questions to Build Anticipation

Asking young people questions about their lives, hopes, and dreams can build anticipation before reading that promotes curiosity, inquisitiveness, suspense, predictability, and above all, engagement. Asking students to invest of themselves prior to reading—and throughout the reading experience itself—encourages young people (and their teachers) to assume a more personal and self-invested role in the learning experience. Too often, educators concentrate on facts, vocabulary, and dramatic structure, when these learning outcomes will naturally present themselves if the student is invested in the story. Prior to reading *Drama High*, teachers can ask several questions about theater and the general framework of the book:

- Have you ever been to the theater?
- What plays have you seen performed? Where?
- Have you ever met a famous actor or actress? Who do you idolize? What would you do if that person walked into the room right now?
- Who is the person you would be most surprised to see at our school?
- What would make a celebrity interested in visiting our school?
- What teacher or adult serves as a role model to you? In what way does he or she inspire you?
- What extracurricular activity do you enjoy, and what life skills have you learned through participating in that activity?

Spectrum of Difference

The Spectrum of Difference (Neelands & Goode, 2015) is a quick activity to find out where students stand on an issue. Using masking or painter's tape, the teacher creates a long line across the classroom floor. With one side of the line representing "strongly agree," the other side representing "strongly disagree," and the middle "neutral," the teacher reads statements to encourage healthy debate. Students can first move to the place along the line that represents their individual points of view, and volunteers may share why they chose their position. Statements related to *Drama High* might include,

- High school theater is not as good as professional theater;
- High school students should only perform shows written for high schools;
- Students participating in high school extracurricular opportunities should be trained like and treated like professionals; or
- Extracurricular activities are just for fun.

Make Predictions

Pre-reading activities can extend beyond personal revelation and preferences to actual narrative prediction and assumptions. By asking students to predict what *Drama High* might be about, teachers are encouraging students to summon their knowledge, experience, and imagination to speculate what might happen in the nonfiction text they are about to read. Correlating with the literacy standards for collaboration and writing, teachers can ask their students to write predictive responses to questions that ask them to anticipate what they

might be reading about in this nonfiction work. From reading the title alone—
*Drama High: The Incredible True Story of a Brilliant Teacher, a Struggling
Town, and the Magic of Theater*—students can easily be asked these questions:

- What do you think this book is about?
- What makes for a brilliant teacher?
- What is meant by a struggling town?
- Why is theater considered magical?
- Why do you think the author wrote this book?

These kinds of questions help students prepare future responses in which they
can write narratives to develop real or imagined experiences or events using
effective technique, well-chosen details, and well-structured even sequences.

Use Creative Drama Activities

Pre-reading activities do not need to be confined to only reading, writing, and
speaking tasks. To be sure, all are essential and meet national standards, but
students can also benefit from the imaginative, physical, emotional, and collaborative components of theater exercises. Any pre-reading activity could involve
creative drama, defined as the process-based exploration of a text-based or
imagined scenario, often rooted in improvisation and guided by a facilitator.
These creative drama activities to prepare students to read *Drama High* reinforce the representation of a subject or a key scene in two different mediums
and how different scenes create very different perspectives on the plot.

Tableau

Again considering the title of the book, students can work in small groups
of four to six participants to develop a tableau—a frozen image using their
bodies, spatial relationships, and facial expressions—illustrating what they
predict the book will be about. When students share their tableaux, have
observers reflect on what they see and consider the similarities and differences among groups.

Pantomime

Have students think about an extracurricular activity or hobby of which they
are most passionate (a sport, art form, etc.) in order to improvise a short solo
pantomime (in which they hold and manipulate imaginary objects without
speaking) as though they are preparing for the activity. Encourage students
to consider what they are thinking and feeling as they prepare. After rehears-
ing independently, students can volunteer to perform. Watching two or three

pantomimes will allow the class to see parallels in what students are doing and feeling, leading into a discussion about the ways in which extracurricular activities are important to high school students.

Vocabulary of the Theater

Finally, it might behoove students to familiarize themselves with the vocabulary of the theater prior to their reading. Words like *character motivation, intent, super-objective, method acting, upstage, downstage, stage right, stage left, fly area, wings, proscenium, backdrop, mezzanine, balcony,* and *thrust stage* may be defined prior to reading or added to a word wall progressively as students make their way through the text. This correlates with the standards for building vocabulary and asks students to think in a new language—a highly technical language germane to the theater—and one, in which for many students, might be brand new.

WHILE READING *DRAMA HIGH: THE INCREDIBLE TRUE STORY OF A BRILLIANT TEACHER, A STRUGGLING TOWN, AND THE MAGIC OF THEATER*

The layers presented within this text lead to a number of options for activities during students' reading. Teachers can assign this book to be read cover to cover (as most eager high school drama students will do on their own), or they can assign individual passages that highlight Volpe's drama program and his students' passion to perform. In this section, we provide classroom lessons that encourage both and leave it up to the discretion of the teacher as to how best to tackle this frank and inspiring work.

Reading Aloud

During the reading, students can read aloud passages of particular interest. Since this book is recommended for high school drama classes, it is only fitting that students should be reading aloud, practicing their speaking voice and their ability to convey meaning with their best interpretive and analytical skills. Reading aloud can be done in partners, small groups, and/or in whole-class settings, as each requires the reader to adjust their voice and volume to the exigencies of the given arrangement.

Performing a Scene

Inviting students to perform excerpts from plays mentioned in the text will allow them to immerse themselves in their reading and see firsthand how vivid these stage dramas are in depicting the human condition, while simultaneously sharing these scenes with their fellow students. Teachers can reinforce their reading—and classroom presentations—by highlighting the scene performances with discussions, questions, and follow-up writing assignments.

Another option is to have students imagine how Volpe was received as a new teacher at Truman High. Was he met with immediate acceptance? Did anyone question or challenge his choices? Have students develop two-person improvised scenes with one student in the role as Volpe and the other student in the role as teacher, administrator, community member, or student; and present the conflict that might emerge between these two characters, their points of view, and how they navigate the conflict.

Living Sculpture

Ask students to compile a list of themes from *Drama High* that occur during their reading: youth empowerment, coming of age, collaboration, inspiration, creative expression, overcoming odds, and legacy are possibilities. In the Living Sculpture activity (Neelands & Goode, 2015), one student serves as a "sculptor" for this exercise and chooses additional students to serve as her or his "clay." The sculptor guides the clay into a tableau to represent one of the themes; he or she may verbally direct the clay on how to move, gently guide the clay using physical touch, or may demonstrate for the clay the physicality and facial expressions he or she would like them to portray. Once the sculptor has completed the tableau, the teacher can guide a discussion about what the sculptor has created, soliciting observations, emotional responses, and parallels between what students see and the themes presented in *Drama High*. Students may also offer suggestions on how to adjust the tableau to clarify or strengthen the image, or to offer a different perspective on the same theme.

AFTER READING *DRAMA HIGH: THE INCREDIBLE TRUE STORY OF A BRILLIANT TEACHER, A STRUGGLING TOWN, AND THE MAGIC OF THEATER*

Writing Activities

After reading *Drama High*, students need the chance to illustrate their understanding of the book's key thematic ideas as well as the content of the nonfiction narrative. In addition to culminating writing activities, students can engage in a whole range of exercises involving reading, speaking, and drawing. These lessons will help students share their knowledge of their reading, their understanding of theater, and the exigencies of the human condition.

Culminating writing activities might ask students to contemplate the following questions:

- What did you learn about Harry S. Truman High School? What kind of students attend? What is the high school like? The community? Does it sound familiar? Why?
- What did you learn about Mr. Volpe, the drama teacher? What kind of teacher is he? Do you admire him? Do you know teachers like Mr. Volpe? Explain.
- Volpe is openly gay and encourages his students to embrace their own sexuality. What risks is Volpe taking with this choice, and how does this aspect of his teaching methodology impact his students? Do you agree with Volpe's position on this subject matter? Why or why not?
- Mr. Volpe's students perform edgy, true-to-life dramas. How do students feel about producing plays for a high school audience and the broader community where the language and contact can often be raw, harsh, and real? Do they believe that high school students should openly tackle subjects—like rape and abuse and drugs—in a dramatic form for all to see, or are these topics best discussed in private where trusted adults can best monitor discussions that can often become heated and volatile? Would you like to perform in these kind of plays? Why?

  - *Spring Awakening* is a musical about adolescent sexuality. Would you perform in such a play? Why or why not?
  - *Good Boys or True* is a drama about a girl who is sexually abused and a boy who is charged with her abuse. Is this topic relevant for today's teens?

- Many of Mr. Volpe's students graduate and become theater professionals, but many do not. Would you like to work in the theater? Why or why not? What skills developed in the theater classroom are valuable in other professions?
- Mr. Volpe's drama students work long and rigorous hours to develop their skills and mount high quality theater. What motivates them to work so hard? What in your life motivates you to work hard?

Creative Drama Activities

Creative drama is the one activity where students can simultaneously think on their feet and write in their heads. Not dependent on script and/or facts, creative drama allows participants to actively engage in improvisational acting within the framework provided by the teacher. Contrary to popular misconceptions, creative drama is not a free for all but rather a carefully sculpted classroom experience in which individuals can express creatively and openly their understandings of a given situation. And in the case of the *Drama High* narrative—where improvisational acting plays a prominent role in both rehearsals and performance—creative drama becomes the perfect venue for students to define and explore what they read. Dramatic performances provide students with the opportunity to do both on-task student talk and physical movement. This type of talk and movement allow for students to create new meanings, new texts, and ultimately a stronger literacy community (Clark, 2012). "By considering dramatic performance as a strategy for inquiry and/or for drafting," writes Clark, "students become better speakers and language users" (p. 65).

Beyond writing, theatrical exercises can help students reflectively respond to a text, allowing them to more deeply explore their ideas, their values, and their perspectives. Creating intersections between students' academic and personal lives through honest and open conversations related to a reading expands their social, emotional, and moral development (Bernier, Carlson, & Whipple, 2010). Fostering these connections is the heart of strong instructional practices, and theater provides ample opportunity for such engagement. Students who have just finished reading portions or the entire text of *Drama High* should have the opportunity to reflect on the text in a variety of modes.

Forum Theater

A Forum Theater (Boal, 2002) has students identify moments where a character in *Drama High* was oppressed: an administrator controlling Volpe's show selections or teaching methodology; a parent telling a child that he or she can no longer do theater because he or she needs to work to help support the family; or one student threatening another in an attempt to keep him or her from auditioning for the lead role. Then, volunteers improvise a scene to play out the conflict, one which cannot be resolved. The teacher pauses the performance and asks for suggestions on different choices that the oppressed character could make to try to be free of this oppression. As students in the audience make suggestions, they may then "tap into" the scene, replacing the actor playing the oppressed character. As students become familiar with this format, they may also "tap into" other scenes and try different ways to heighten the conflict.

Monologues

Ask students to prepare and present a short improvised monologue about a specific individual from *Drama High*. Voicing a character allows students to share their impressions about how an individual contributes to the story's narrative. This exercise allows students to internalize their reading in a manner that is more open and immediate than mere writing can reveal. Teachers may wish to allow time for students to select, prepare, and define their character impersonations prior to presenting them, as their preparation will reinforce their need to be careful in their selection of who and what they want to present. Moreover, we encourage teachers to have students work from just an outline so they are not just reading word for word what an individual said in their reading but rather internalizing and verbalizing their ideas, opinions, and emotions.

Reunion Improvisation

Ask students to imagine they are attending a reunion and/or retirement party for Mr. Volpe at Truman High. At the event, students take turns sharing what shows were the most meaningful to them and why, favorite memories or inside jokes, and what they learned from Volpe and one another. Students can make toasts in honor of Volpe, and after the toasts the guest of honor (a brave student playing the part of Volpe) can offer a speech. Following this improvisation, students can reflect on how the characters' perspectives shifted with the passing of time.

Walls Have Ears

In Walls Have Ears (Neelands & Goode, 2015), students line up shoulder-to-shoulder in two lines as though they are in a long hallway. Have a student volunteer step into the role as Sokolove returning to the hallways of Harry S. Truman High School. As Sokolove walks down the hallway, what "voices" does he hear from his memories as a high school student? The students who represent the wall speak as those voices, saying quotes from the text or improvised lines that capture the multiple memories and people Sokolove encountered as a theater student. Alternatively, Sokolove can walk down the hall in the opposite direction, representing the completion of his research for his book. Now that he has grown up and experienced his high school theater program as a journalist, what new voices, personalities, and perspectives can be added to the mix? These juxtaposing improvisations can open up the potential for reflective dialogue about how writing the book changed or strengthened Sokolove's perspective of his town, high school, teacher, and theater.

EXTENSION ACTIVITIES BEYOND *DRAMA HIGH: THE INCREDIBLE TRUE STORY OF A BRILLIANT TEACHER, A STRUGGLING TOWN, AND THE MAGIC OF THEATER*

Given the time and space to further expand on the themes presented in *Drama High*, students can turn to the arts—music, dance, visual arts, and theater—to make a difference in their own community. As Volpe remarks, if all "we had was a bare stage with one light bulb, we could still do theatre." With this sentiment, students can explore how they might become advocates for the arts in education regardless of budgetary constraints or lack of resources. What follows is a list of activities that can exemplify and underline students' knowledge and understanding of the book *Drama High*:

- Develop an original play or work of art that features social justice themes relevant to your community.
- Create posters with inspirational quotes and visual art (either from *Drama High* or other sources) to display around campus.
- Design and produce a PowerPoint or short movie to promote your own high school theater program using class or production photos, student quotes, and selected music. This video may be shared with administrators, the student body, or the community via social media to share the impact of arts education.
- Invite local theater or entertainment professionals who work in the industry to share their life and perspectives. Meeting individuals who work in the arts can help students appreciate both the artistic and utilitarian nature of this changing and dynamic profession.
- Organize a fine arts fair, open to all high school students and their parents, where students can receive information on how to get involved in arts organizations on campus. If possible, arts organizations can display work or perform at this event.
- Visit local elementary or middle schools to facilitate theater exercises, direct a simple play, or share a youth-appropriate performance.
- Prepare monologues, poems, or excerpts from plays, novels, and/or speeches as "Actors for Hire." Then, when requested, students can deliver these performances to other classes in their school. For example, students studying World War II might be treated to an excerpt read by Winston Churchill himself; or students studying poetry might be entertained by visit from Emily Dickinson or Robert Frost.

CONCLUSION

Drama High provides adolescents many avenues to learn about theater as both a vocation and an avocation. This book also provides opportunities for students to acquire knowledge and develop skills in both theater and the English language arts. The narrative of this nonfiction work—a journalist's return to his former high school to pay homage to his theater teacher—offers an accessible platform for both content teachers to integrate written, spoken, and artistic expression in their classrooms. Students can utilize both literacy activities and theater to enhance their understanding of their own passions and aspirations. Yes, students can learn to be analytical in their thinking, critical in their reading, and practical in their analysis, but the exploration of this book can also pave the way for creative and honest self-expression. Students can discuss how the world of theater can directly relate and respond to the world of social issues—and more importantly, to students' immediate lives and concerns. For in *Drama High*, students learn how social issues can be dramatically portrayed and how art—and the learning of one's craft—can transform lives.

As this chapter has demonstrated, writing lessons are essential for helping adolescents develop their critical thinking skills and language fluency. Writing allows students to focus and hone their thinking as students must wrestle with word choice, sentence structure, and contextual meaning. For these reasons, we suggest that writing be incorporated in all subject areas, including theater. Students can keep journals, logs, and/or critical commentaries before, during, and after their reading so as to prompt even longer and involved writing pieces. Helping students sharpen their thinking on paper provides them with the foundation to collect their thoughts, organize their impressions, recall specific instances in the reading that were the most vivid, define their understanding, and think analytically about the implications of what they have read.

Annotated List of Related YA Literature

Drama by Raina Telgemeir (240 pp.)

Drama is a graphic novel that depicts the life of twelve-year-old Callie, an aspiring thespian who tries out for the middle school production of *Moon over Mississippi* even though she can't sing. Instead, she volunteers to design the play's scenery, which leads to all sorts of complications from no money, an uncooperative stage crew, and egocentric actors—all resulting in hilarious middle-school mishaps told in cartoonish pictures and easy-to-read dialogue.

The Truth about My Success by Dyan Sheldon (351 pp.)

Paloma Rose is a sixteen-year-old starlet who has her own television show and millions of adoring fans. Trouble is, stardom has gone to her head, and her scandalous behavior threatens to upend her fame and fortune. Her mother and her agent in an act of intervention send her off to a ranch for troubled teens where she is brought back to earth. Meanwhile, a double is hired to replace Paloma on her TV show, and, as you can imagine, more trouble ensues.

Talent by B. Lynn Goodwin (292 pp.)

Fifteen-year-old Sandee Mason copes with fear and anxiety through her involvement in the high school theater club after she loses her big brother, Bri; he has disappeared while serving in Afghanistan.

My Life: The Musical by Maryrose Wood (240 pp.)

Phillip and Emily, two teens from Long Island, become obsessed with a Broadway musical, *Aurora*. Together, they see every performance they can until the show eventually takes over their lives. Together they go to hilarious lengths to indulge their theatrical passion.

Taking Flight: From War Orphan to Star Ballerina by Michaela DePrince and Elaine DePrince (256 pp.)

In this engaging memoir a young orphan, who was tormented for a skin condition while living in a West African orphanage, is adopted by an American family. Her new family encourages and nurtures her love of ballet, and now she is an international star ballerina.

The Fall Musical (Drama Club #1) by Peter Lerangis (214 pp.)

For the teens at Ridgefield High in Long Island, the drama club is everything. There, teens learn to navigate the allure of the stage with the drama that occurs behind the scenes.

REFERENCES

Bernier, A., Carlson, S., & Whipple, N. (2010). From external regulation to self-regulation: Early parenting precursors of young children's executive functioning. *Child Development, 81*(1), 326–339.

Boal, A. (2002). *Games for actors and non-actors* (2nd ed.). London, UK: Routledge.

Clark, S. (2012). Guiding the noticing: Using a dramatic performance experience to promote tellability in narrative writing. *Clearing House, 85*(2), 65–69.

DePrince, M., & DePrince, E. (2014). *Taking flight: From war orphan to star ballerina*. New York: Random House.

Goodwin, B. L. (2015). *Talent*. Madison, WI: Caliburn Press, LLC.

Lerangis. P. (2007). *The fall musical (drama club #1)*. New York: Speak.

Neelands, J., & Goode, T. (2015). *Structuring drama work: 100 key conventions for theatre and drama* (3rd ed.). Cambridge, UK: Cambridge University Press.

Sheldon, D. (2015). *The truth about my success*. Somerville, MA: Candlewick Press.

Sokolove, M. (2013). *Drama high: The incredible true story of a brilliant teacher, a struggling town, and the magic of theater*. New York: Riverhead Books.

Telgemeir, R. (2012). *Drama*. New York: Scholastic.

Wood, M. (2008). *My life: The musical*. New York: Delacorte Books for Young Readers.

Chapter 12

A Music and ELA Project: Connections through Brendan Kiely's *The Last True Love Story*

Steven T. Bickmore and Isaac Bickmore

Music surrounds our earliest education: parents sing lullabies; grandparents often add songs from different eras or cultures; and little children learn the lyrics and motions of *Itsy Bitsy Spider*, the *Hokey Pokey*, and *Ring around the Rosy*. We maintain that this is an early introduction to music and literacy. Many American children have their introduction to letters through the *Alphabet Song*, and we know that a single letter can represent several sounds. As a result, early childhood educators often use music to introduce more complex phonemic awareness (Chappel, 2008; Dyer, 2011; Iwasaki, Rasinski, Yildirim, & Zimmerman, 2013). A quick web search will produce websites replete with songs for teaching literacy.

Considering music's versatility, it is amazing how infrequently music is included as a catalyst for inquiry in the curriculum of other secondary subjects. We situate the project in an ELA class but encourage adaptation in other contexts. In other words, music can serve ELA and ELA can serve music. This principle may be best embodied by Bob Dylan's music and lyrics. Dylan's work is important in Kiely's novel, *The Last True Love Story*; musical references are not just to enhance mood but are an integral component of plot, character development, and mood. Our chapter could be implemented in a music class, an English language arts (ELA) class, or as a collaboration between disciplines. We adhere to project-based learning models, inspired by Dewey (1938) and Piaget (1969) that transcend class boundaries.

THE LAST TRUE LOVE STORY BY BRENDAN KIELY (288 PP.)

Any novel containing the phrase, "I need to get to Ithaca" (p. 50) should pluck the heartstrings of any English teacher. Homer's odyssey, Huck Finn's journey, Ignatius J. Reilly's ramblings through New Orleans, Marlow's journey into the legendary heart of darkness, Paul Berlin's mythical chase after Cacciato, and Milkman's wanderings through the pages of Morrison's *Song of Solomon* all conjure up a journey motif. While differing in context, their guides, their missteps, and their wanderings, all bear signposts that mark the journey: islands and sirens, towns and charlatans, the wayward journey of a hot dog cart, the chugging of a steam engine, rice paddies, or mythical flights.

In Kiely's *The Last True Love Story*, the protagonist Teddy Hendrix is on a mission to escort his grandfather home, and their journey is punctuated by songs played along the highway from Malibu to Ithaca. Their trek is marked by conversations referencing musicians and songs that provide context, characterization, and commentary. It is Corrina, Teddy's love interest and her influence, that makes music the nuanced focus of meaning and interpretation. Corrina, the adopted Guatemalan daughter of ex-hippies, plays either her guitar or her playlist providing the right song for the moment.

"Hey," [Teddy] said. "Let's just choose one and stick with it."
"Nope," Corrina shot back. "I gotta find something to fit the mood right now."
"What's our mood right now?"
"I don't know. But I'll know it when I hear it." (p. 69)

Corrina, named after a Dylan song, is not just channeling her parents' "oldies"; she is a poetic oracle following another namesake, Corrina, a Greek female poet from the fifth century. Grandpa a.k.a. Gpa corrects Teddy when he calls Corrina's selections "oldies."

"I mean, they named me after a Bob Dylan song they loved, so there's that."
"And then what? They drilled you on oldies for the rest of your life?"
"Classic," Gpa said from the back.
"What?"
"Classic rock," he said. "Don't call it oldie."
"Yeah, Hendrix," Corrina teased. "It's classic." She laughed and then sang along with the song, her voice looping, harmonizing with the vocals coming out of the speakers. (p. 81)

Hendrix's grandfather is in the declining stages of Alzheimer's, and Hendrix hopes to escort his father back to Ithaca, where Gpa met, fell in love, and lived with his late wife Betty, before he can no longer conjure up her memory. Gpa is already having trouble; memories come and go, and he can get angry. As the journey progresses, it is Corrina's music—music she selects from her phone or plays on her guitar—that calms Gpa. Music stimulates his memory. The songs bring memories of specific events with Betty, his wife and Hendrix's Gma. Hendrix then adds stories to the Hendrix Family Book (HFB), which, in turn, helps him locate his own identity. Gpa and his piecemeal stories are Hendrix's final connection to his dead father. As a result, Hendrix, Gpa, and Corrina experience an intergenerational musical journey to explore Gpa's memory, Hendrix's self-discovery, and Corrina's potential as a poetic oracle and professional musician.

Kiely's wonderful novel contributes to our project in several ways: The novel provides a means (1) to connect to coming-of-age themes and a journey connecting classical mythology, the Vietnam War, and the counterculture of the 1960s; (2) to engage musically with those themes; (3) to learn and engage with principles of songwriting; and (4) to help students think critically about how music and literature function in their lives.

CONNECTING (HARMONIZING) MUSIC AND LITERACY

While mixing music and the ELA, we favor instruction that looks at the whole unit in a harmonious way. Planning for standards to be met from both subject areas can be introduced systematically in a manner that scaffolds student learning within each unit and throughout the school year. As a result, any individual unit may cover several standards from both concentrations while specifically focusing on a few. The 2014 National Core Arts Standards (NCAS) were recently reorganized using a framework developed by Grant Wiggins and Jay McTighe (2005). These guidelines are comprised of eleven anchor standards divided into four arts processes: Creating, Performing/Presenting/Producing, Responding, and Connecting. In our chapter, students will engage in a series of creative musical activities before, during, and after reading *The Last True Love Story*. The activities involve aspects of songwriting using free web apps, ukuleles and guitars, and other online resources. All activities align with NCAS and involve pre-, during-, and post-activities that deepen students' understanding of the book.

Next, we focus on the ELA standards as a teacher creates a unit integrating both music and the English language arts. We suggest using Kiely's novel in the context of a project to help students engage standard themes of coming of age and the archetypal journey that connect to classical mythology, the Vietnam War, and the counterculture of the 1960s, engage musically with many of those themes, learn and engage with principles of songwriting, and help students think critically about how music and literature function in their lives (Frith, 1987).

SONGWRITING PROJECT: AN INTEGRATED
MUSIC AND ELA PROJECT

The Last True Love Story Songwriting Project is a series of before during and after activities and small projects designed for a secondary ELA class that is reading Kiely's novel but is flexible enough for use in a general music course or a middle or high school choir. Kiely's book provides an opportunity to learn by engaging in music or songwriting. Think of it as a "choose your own adventure" project where students may make changes suited to their personal tastes. This interdisciplinary project engages students in activities that address the themes, characters, and settings from the book through musical and writing activities. Throughout the project, students will showcase their work: performing original songs; playing prerecorded original songs; describing how the songs represent or draw on the themes, characters, and settings of the book; and also describing the technical and musical skills gained as a result of engaging in the process. Students, in small groups or by themselves, will study key elements and themes in the novel and engage in musical activities that reinforce them. Some class time will be provided for each, but mastery may require time beyond class. Each group will select an activity from each category. For more resources visit Steve's website here: http://www.yawednesday.com/music-and-ya.html.

BEFORE READING *THE LAST TRUE LOVE STORY*

We recommend that teachers read the book before attempting this project with students. While reading, teachers are advised to make a list of all songs and musical artists that are referenced. To introduce the book, ask students to write what they know about the Beatles and other groups from the 1960s. Once completed, assign one or both of these assignments to student groups.

Learn to Play a Song

Using ukuleles, guitars, or a mobile instrument app, learn one of the songs referenced in the novel. This is a perfect opportunity for you to collaborate with the music teacher for instruction and use of instruments. Students will need to research and practice. We recommend the online tutorials of "The Ukulele Teacher" (n.d.) for help learning to play the ukulele and particularly the You Tube video "How to Tune a Ukulele!" for help. Each group will perform for the class and all members must participate in some way.

Research Presentation

Students research a musical group discussed in the book and prepare a five-minute research presentation using visual media, audio examples, and connections to literature that accomplish their message. Have them prepare a list of the resources they used and individually, prepare an explanation of what was learned. For example students might address the following in their individual explanations: (1) student's level of participation, (2) student's new understanding of the musical group, (3) the research process, and (4) the tools each student used.

WHILE READING *THE LAST TRUE LOVE STORY*

We encourage teachers to do and share these projects along with their students. In that way, teachers are fully aware of the benefits of using these assignments.

Character Playlist

Make a playlist for characters in the book. Each group member selects one character and creates a playlist of ten songs that demonstrate the character's development by capturing the moods, emotions, changes, actions, and ideas displayed in the narrative while reading. Have them present their projects via a YouTube channel, a web page, a PowerPoint with links, a Prezi, or a Spotify playlist. There will be a project day at the end of the unit that might resemble an exposition with multiple presentations at different stations. Each group can take turns presenting while the rest serve as an audience along with other invited guests—parents, other classes, school and district administrators, and so on.

Character Mashup

Ask students to choose two characters from *The Last True Love Story* and find a song that best represents each of them. It could be a song from the novel or a song they know from their own lives that fits the character. Then have students search for a mashup of those songs online. If no mashup exists, then ask them to describe why they think two certain songs would work well together. (Students with more advanced music and technology skills might even create a new mashup.) If a mashup exists, have students describe how the different musical and lyrical elements of each song work together.

The best way to do this is to play a portion of the first song, and as it plays, describe the elements that you think are similar to the other song. Point your audience toward the musical elements that will work with the other song. Then, play the other song and do the same as you did for the first song. The last step is to play the mashup. Finally, have students describe the relationship dynamic between the two characters, including how they interact with each other and how students think they feel about each other. Make sure students provide evidence from the book to support their viewpoints.

AFTER READING *THE LAST TRUE LOVE STORY*

An ELA teacher, well versed in the implementation of standards, will see how these projects allow students to explore both the elements of fiction and music as they craft work that demonstrates an understanding and a mastery of both curricula.

Mood, Tone, and Music

Assign specific chapters to groups. For each chapter, students select a song that represents the theme, tone, or mood of the chapter.

Write a Song

Ask students to write and record a song based on the themes, characters, or setting of the book, using any available resource to accomplish this such as a Smartphone with apps and/or computer tools such as Soundation, Soundtrap, or Garage Band. Have them refer to online tutorials and online help services to answer any questions. Students can also record themselves playing and singing. Check out "Tech-Based Composing Demystified," a plethora of tech tools developed by Jesse Rathgeber (2014) to enhance creative composition experiences for students.

Turn Hendrix's Poem into a Song

Students might take Hendrix's poem for Gpa (p. 274) and set it to music. Consider these two options: (1) Students find a simple three chord song on the Internet that they could sing Hendrix's lyrics over while playing it on the ukulele, or (2) set up a loop arrangement on Soundtrap and sing the lyrics over the top of the loops. Students may modify the lyrics to fit the rhythm of the music if appropriate. Dylan, Morrison, and other musicians often modify their own lyrics in live performance.

Create Corrina's First Album Cover and Liner Notes

In groups, students design a full album for Corrina considering these questions:

• What would be the title of her first album?
• Imagine the titles of the songs. Would she do covers or would they all be originals?
• Where would she record it? L.A.? New York? Nashville?
• What musicians would she hire to record with?
• Design the album's cover art.
• Imagine and include ten song titles and assign authorship.

Examples may be found at "The Liner Note Project." In addition, Portman's *King Dork* (2006) has good examples of this activity. If a student chose to write a song for the first activity in this section, it could be one of the songs on Corrina's album.

EXTENSION ACTIVITIES BEYOND *THE LAST TRUE LOVE STORY*

Everyone Embodies a Musical History

Without a doubt Gpa has a musical history. His memory is enhanced by the music that surrounds him on their trip. Corrina, as an oracle, provides Gpa a soundtrack to choose from. I (Isaac) once conducted a narrative study of Billy Cioffi who told me that he was the history of Rock n' Roll. Is Billy's claim serious? Is it bravado, is it a way to take the air out of a room, or is it an expression of how he understands his life? While I believe it is the latter, how can Billy's claim be applied to anyone? Am I the history of rock and roll? Is my father? Are you? In my own experience, I grew up listening to my parents' music: Elton John, The Beatles, The Temptations, Creedence Clearwater Revival, Joni Mitchell, Aretha Franklin, James Brown, James Taylor, Van Morrison, the Rolling Stones, the Talking Heads, and so on. Music was a constant presence in our home. We listened to music as we cleaned on Saturday mornings. I scrubbed the bathtub and found out that "Elbow Grease" wasn't the name of a cleaner, while Mick Jagger explained that *You Can't Always Get What You Want*.

In adolescence, I loved the Spin Doctors, Boys II Men, Aerosmith, Blues Travelers, Marvin Gaye, Stevie Wonder, Lauryn Hill, and so on. I listened to most of this on compact discs. While listening, I also engaged with music in different contexts. I had a year of piano lessons, and I started writing songs using a ukulele that my grandfather gave me. This music is part of me; I experienced it and lived it. The music wrapped around my memories. When I hear the songs now, they mark the passing of time. Some help me look inward, but others help me look outward, forward, and backward. I manage my personal and social life with help from those songs. Listening to some songs help me feel a sense of ownership and belonging (Frith, 1987). I have embodied a musical history of popular music and live a life deeply affected by rock and roll. No doubt, my rock and roll history will be different than yours. It is tied to my mother's stories of listening to Joni Mitchell albums for the first time, and it is this history that attaches my personal experience to songs. An embodied history is by necessity a personal history.

In *A People's History of The United States* by Howard Zinn (1997), the arrival of Columbus is told from the point of view of native peoples who were massacred. It makes all the difference. From Columbus' point of view, the one most often studied in school, you understand the Americas as a discovery. On the other hand, from the indigenous point of view, you see the Americas as part of an active and ancient civilization that is invaded. Zinn's text flips the story, forcing us to think of history from a different perspective, from a different field of constitution and validity.

What if we took it one step further?

Zinn's history flips the perspective on historical events and retells the stories from a different point of view, but it is still a chronological history. What if we decided to write a people's history of rock and roll that wasn't necessarily chronological but more embodied? Where would we start? An embodied history of rock and roll might be told from the point of view of a thirteen-year-old girl with whom I did a research project. I gave her an iPod and asked her to make movies about her musical life. She made videos with her baby brother dancing to her favorite songs. She made videos of herself and her friends dancing to "Watch Me Whip" and "Hit the Kwan."

What does her musical engagement have to do with the history of rock and roll? A host of songs introduce, or reintroduce, a certain type of dance: the Twist, the Locomotion, the Electric Slide, the Boot Scootin' Boogie, the Hustle, the Macarena, Teach Me How to Dougie, the Call of the Jitterbug, Land of a Thousand Dances, and others. More recent songs in that list have music videos that show (teach) the dance. For example, the video "Teach Me How to Jerk" by Audio Push is set in a school. The opening scene features a teacher who is obviously boring, and the students act as bored students do. The teacher gives up and says, "All right. You guys don't want to listen to this stuff. Octane, why don't you come and teach the class?" At that point Octane, one half of the group Audio Push, comes to the front of the room and the music starts. "Won't you 'Teach Me How to Jerk' "? The rest of the video features students dancing all over the school, demonstrating different versions of a dance.

The project referenced before of the girl using her iPod to make her own videos is not the only teenager to have done this. A YouTube search using the term, "Watch me whip fan videos" yielded 702,000 results, many made by teenagers. As Zinn has written a people's history of the United States by shifting the point of view, one could write a teenager's history of rock and roll by doing the same. If there were no adolescents with time and money to spend on recordings, would we know about Elvis Presley? Would there be a top 40?

Personal Musical History

Have students, like the girl with the iPod, use their smart phones to make their own movies about their musical lives. Or, if you prefer, have each student write a personal musical history using ten songs. These songs might be from the radio, television, family activities, the neighborhood, church activities, or musicals. They should share them in some presentation format. A written explanation may or may not be required.

My Musical Family Tree

This is similar to the Personal Musical History except that students focus on how family members have contributed music to their lives. Refer to the music history section of the chapter.

Music as a Historical Marker

Introduce how music can be representative of different moments in history. To develop this idea, students can work in groups that explore the popular songs in the decades that span the ages of the characters in the book. They can discuss in which communities these songs were popular, do they connect to specific dances, political movements, and so on.

Musical Allusions

Select a musical allusion from each chapter and research the cultural and historical position of the reference.

CONCLUSION

Boundaries between disciplines should blur. Having a bit of musical chaos/ creation in the classroom is a wonderful exploration of cross-curricular collaboration. Perhaps the kids with earphones draped over their shoulders would take the lead instead of glaring from the back row with an angst ridden stare. If we really want to communicate with all students, we might try harder to reach them where their interests lie. Engaging musically with our text selection serves as a model for a large number of YA texts that a student might encounter and teachers can use to connect music and YA literature (Bickmore, 2017). Since a teenager's relationship to music is fertile ground for learning, ask students to visually or sonically display the ways they interact with their own music and create their own music histories. There are many other connections that can be made with YA fiction that feature popular music as a theme (Bickmore & Bickmore, 2016).

Annotated List of Related YA Literature

The Haters by Jesse Andrews (325 pp.)

Sixteen-year-olds Wes and Corey have been friends since middle school. Their love of music, specifically jazz, has created a lifelong bond between the two. During the summer before their junior year in high school, a girl named Ash tests the strength of their friendship. While participating in Bill Garabedian's Jazz Giants of Tomorrow Intensive Summer Workshop, Ash convinces the boys to form a three-member band and tour the country. As they travel across the southern United States in search of venues to play, we not only meet people they encounter along the way, but we learn how each happenstance leaves them learning something new about themselves and each other. From Tennessee to Louisiana, "The Haters Summer Tour of Hate 2016" would prove to be more of a self-exploration tour than a musical one. For in the end, Wes, Corey, and Ash discover that even though they all come from different walks of life, they have more than just music in common.

Nick and Norah's Infinite Playlist by Rachel Cohn
and David Levithan (183 pp.)

Nick is a bassist in a band who happens to be playing a gig at a punk rock club. Everything is going great, until his ex shows up and he becomes desperate to save face in front of her and her new boyfriend. Nora, the daughter of a record company CEO, just happens to be standing there. Nick turns and asks Nora to be his five-minute girlfriend. From that point on, Nick and Norah recognize the chemistry between them, but their feelings are compromised by their previous relationships.

Breakout by Kevin Emerson (304 pp.).

Anthony, an overweight angry eighth grader, feels like everyone is against him. The only thing that makes him feel better is playing in his rock band. But when he writes a song about how he feels for Family Arts Night, someone records it and it goes viral, giving Anthony celebrity status. But when he has to actually perform it in front of a live audience, will he have the nerve to sing it exactly like he wrote it?

King Dork by Frank Portman (368 pp.)

Tom Henderson is a typical high school sophomore. He is smart but puts forth little effort. His father died in the line of duty, but the circumstances surrounding hid death are a mystery that Tom hopes to solve. When he finds his dad's copy of *The Catcher in the Rye*, his world is turned upside down. Suddenly high school gets more complicated. Portman wrote a sequel to this novel, *King Dork Approximately* (2014).

Eleanor and Park by Rainbow Rowell (336 pp.)

The two could not have been more different. Even so Eleanor, the new girl, and Park, a local, are bound together by music. The music heard on Parks' Walkman tells their story.

REFERENCES

Andrews, J. (2016). *The haters*. New York: Abrams.

Bickmore, S. T. (2017, January 27). *Music and YA literature as a natural point of collaboration* (web post). Retrieved from http://www.yawednesday.com/music-and-ya.html.

Bickmore, S. T., & Bickmore, I. L. (2016). Music and the young adult novel: Assessing how adolescents "read" the music of their lives. In J. Hayn, J. S. Kaplan, & K. R. Clemmons (Eds.), *Teaching young adult literature today: Insights, considerations, and perspectives for the classroom teacher* (2nd ed.), 149–174. Lanham, MD: Rowman & Littlefield.

Chappell, J. (2008). The link between music and literacy. *Teaching music, 15*(5), 46–46.

Cohn, R., & Levithan, D. (2006). *Nick and Nora's infinite playlist*. New York: Knopf Books.

Dewey, J. (1938). *Logic: The theory of inquiry*. New York: Holt and Co.

Dyer, J. L. (2011). Musical thought: Using music to enhance literacy instruction. *Illinois Reading Council Journal, 39*(4), 3–9.

Emmerson, K. (2015). *Breakout*. New York: Crown Books for Young Readers.

Frith, S. (1987). Towards an aesthetic of popular music. In R. D. Leppert & S. McClary (Eds.), *Music and society: The politics of composition, performance and reception*, 133–149. New York: Cambridge University Press.

Iwasaki, B., Rasinski, T., Yildirim, K., & Zimmerman, B. S. (2013). Let's bring back the magic of song for teaching reading. *Reading Teacher, 67*(2), 137–141.

Kiely, B. (2016). *The last true love story*. New York: Margaret K. McElderry Books.

Liner Note Project (n.d.). Retrieved from http://thelinernoteproject.tumblr.com.

Piaget, J. (1969). *Science of education and the psychology of the child*. New York: Viking.

Portman, F. (2008). *King dork*. New York: Delacorte Books.

Rathgeber, J. (2014). *Tech-based composing demystified: Using iPads, computers, and other devices to empower creativity*. NAfME National Conference. Retrieved from http://composingk12.wixsite.com/tech-basedcomposing.

Rowell, R. (2013). *Eleanor and park*. London, UK: St. Martin's Griffin.

The Ukulele Teacher (n.d.). *How to tune a ukulele!* Retrieved from https://www.youtube.com/watch?v=Dl7uzySXUSw.

Wiggins, G. P., & McTighe, J. (2005). *Understanding by design*. Alexandria, VA: Association for Supervision and Curriculum Development.

Zinn, H. (1999). *A people's history of the United States: 1492–present*. New York: Harper Collins.

Chapter 13

YA Sports Literature through a Positive Psychology Framework

Nicole Sieben and Alan Brown

While English language arts (ELA) teachers are often responsible for the integration of literature into secondary school curricula, there are numerous spaces where other content areas could introduce critical works of literature as well. Standards for content literacy requires literature to play a prominent role in student learning through diverse experiences and interactions with a variety of texts that help them to build knowledge, gain insights, explore possibilities, and broaden their perspective. The field of young adult (YA) literature provides one such space for building knowledge, insights, possibilities, and perspectives within the context of a high school psychology classroom. This chapter draws upon a positive psychology framework through which to teach YA literature and navigates the ways in which this can be done using one particular YA novel, *Whale Talk* by Chris Crutcher (2001). What follows is a brief explanation of (a) the positive psychology lens through which this unit can be taught in a psychology course; (b) connection between psychology and literacy in this unit; (c) suggestions for before-reading, during-reading, and after-reading activities as well as extension activities for teaching this book; (d) a list of other YA novels that could be used in ways similar to *Whale Talk*; and (e) conclusions about what this chapter adds to high school curricula.

THROUGH A POSITIVE PSYCHOLOGY LENS

The field of positive psychology offers educators a strengths-based approach to teaching and learning that emphasizes affective dispositions and habits of mind that bring about success for the individual and society (Snyder, Lopez, & Pedrotti, 2011). In this way, positive psychology can offer high school students a space to learn about their own character strengths while simultaneously analyzing the strengths present in characters from certain works of YA literature. According to Peterson and Seligman (2004), there are twenty-four distinct character strengths, and each of these strengths contributes to the success of the individual and the success of a team in unique ways. In order to help students understand how the twenty-four character strengths apply in a person's life and how they can be useful in building skills and other traits, psychology classes can use works of YA literature to demonstrate how certain character strengths can be used as conduits to successful attainment of individual and collective goals.

Peterson and Seligman (2004), often credited as the founders of positive psychology, have developed and refined a valid and reliable survey that measures the degree to which a person possesses and accesses the various strengths in his or her/per life. In their work, Peterson and Seligman have argued that up until the emergence of the relatively new field of positive psychology, there had only been a shared language for speaking about human deficits in psychology, while no such language existed for speaking about human strengths (Snyder et al., 2011). Peterson and Seligman (2004) devised a system for classification and measurement of the twenty-four distinct character strengths, thus providing a means for filling this glaring gap in the field of psychology. The VIA Classification of Virtues and Strengths include twenty-four unique strengths embedded in six categories of virtues. The virtues followed by the strengths included within each category of virtue are (1) wisdom and knowledge—creativity, curiosity, open-mindedness, love of learning, and perspective; (2) courage—bravery, persistence, integrity, and zest; (3) humanity—love, kindness, and social intelligence; (4) justice—citizenship, fairness, and leadership; (5) temperance—forgiveness and mercy, humility, prudence, and self-regulation; and (6) transcendence—appreciation of beauty and excellence, gratitude, hope, humor, and spirituality (Peterson & Seligman, 2004). Helpful infographics of these strengths and their virtue categories for instructional use can be found at the official website of the VIA Institute on Character.

In order to measure these traits accurately, Peterson and Seligman (2004) created an instrument designed to evaluate a person's individual virtues and strengths: the Values in Action Inventory of Strengths (VIA-IS). This survey tool was created to "describe the individual differences of character strengths on a continua and not as distinct categories" (Snyder et al., 2011, p. 48) concerning a person's top strengths of character (not their weaknesses). Through the VIA Survey, "a more strengths-based approach to diagnosis and treatment" and educational interventions became possible (Snyder et al., 2011, p. 46). This survey is available online at the VIA Institute on Character's website (www.viacharacter.org/www/The-Survey) for free and provides survey participants with instant feedback on their character strengths. Teachers can find this survey in two forms: (1) The VIA Survey for Adults and (2) The VIA Survey for Youth. Both surveys rank respondents' twenty-four character strengths based on their level of agreement or disagreement with each of the survey item's statements about their various beliefs, behaviors, and interests.

The survey provides interesting insight into the strengths that each student brings to his or her/per classroom community and can serve as a jumping off point into deeper discussions about contributions to group work, team sports, and other extracurricular activities in a school community. In addition, this focus in a classroom community also serves to meet the goals of high school psychology curricula in the content area standard of *personality* detailed below. Through the model text, *Whale Talk* by Chris Crutcher (2001), we demonstrate the utility of using YA literature in a high school psychology class to teach students about the benefits of building on strengths in each person's personality in order to achieve a "personal best" and "collective good" of a team or other micro or macrocommunity.

WHALE TALK BY CHRIS CRUTCHER (304 PP.)

The Tao (T.J.) Jones, an athletic six-foot-two senior who weighs in at a little under 200 pounds of pure muscle, is a born athlete who excels at every sport he plays. T.J. has never been interested in organized athletics despite the best efforts of high school coaches across various sports, primarily because he has trouble with authority, and most athletics coaches at Cutter High School demand respect whether they have earned it or not. T.J.'s lack of interest in interscholastic sports is best described as a result of what Lipsyte (2011) refers to as jock culture, "a distortion of sports . . . fueled by greed and desperate competition" (para. 6). T.J. describes this culture of sports at Cutter High School in the following way: "Cutter is such a jock school; they pray before games and cajole you to play out of obligation, and fans scream obscenities at one another from the stands, actually creating rivalries between towns, which has always seemed crazy to me" (p. 17).

T.J.'s aversion to sports ends when Mr. Simet, his English teacher, asks for his help forming a swimming team so Simet can avoid being voluntold to coach wrestling, a sport Simet knows nothing about, in favor of swimming, a sport about which he knows a lot as a former Division I college swimmer. T.J. is not all that interested until one day he sees fellow senior Mike Barbour— "[football] linebacker extraordinaire and student most likely to graduate with multiple felonies" (Crutcher, 2001, p. 19)—bullying Chris Coughlin. Chris is a younger student with traumatic brain injury whose older brother (Brian) was a star athlete before being killed tragically during his senior year of high school. Mike chooses to bully Chris for wearing his dead brother's letter jacket, an honor that Mike Barbour believes Chris has not earned. In that moment, T.J. defends Chris, as is his nature, and then and there decides to join Mr. Simet in his quest to recruit enough Cutter High students—athletic or not—to form a swim team that will do just well enough to earn each of them a school letter jacket.

T.J.'s first recruit is Chris Coughlin, and he slowly adds a diverse group of misfits to the mix, including Dan "Never-Use-a-Single-Syllable-When-Polysyllables-Are-Available" Hole (Crutcher, 2001, p. 31); Tay-Roy Kibble, a senior whose dual talents include being a musician and a bodybuilder; Simon DeLong, a 287 pound spectacle of a swimmer; Jackie Craig, a relatively unathletic student just cut from junior varsity football; and Andy Mott, a senior known best for his menacing workout routine and for never talking during the school day.

Over the course of the season, conflicts abound around every corner as T.J. interacts with characters such as Coach Benson, the school's football coach; Mr. Morgan, the school's principal; Rich Marshall, leader of the school's alumni group that supports Cutter's male athletic teams; and, of course, Mike Barbour and his football teammates. How T.J. and his teammates respond to issues of racism, bigotry, and sexual assault in small-town America, and how they come to develop characteristics that include empathy, belonging, and forgiveness are central facets of one of Chris Crutcher's greatest YA novels.

CONNECTING PSYCHOLOGY AND LITERACY

Given the sports literacy focus and team-building emphasis in the storyline, the YA novel, *Whale Talk*, also provides a space for students to discuss relevant aspects of the psychology curricula in meaningful ways. The high school psychology curriculum provides many content standards that allow for the integration of other disciplines as well, including but not limited to ELA literacy standards. The high school psychology curriculum is broken into standard areas, and among these areas is *personality*. The content standards for this area set the goal for students to understand: (1) Perspectives on personality, (2) Assessment of personality, and (3) Issues in personality (National Standards for High School Psychology, 2011). Each content standard area (i.e., *personality*) then includes specific performance standards, which are embedded throughout the chapter. What follows are detailed curricular suggestions for teaching *Whale Talk* through a positive psychology lens, meeting the psychology content standard area of *personality* as well as multiple literacy standards.

Through a conceptual unit grounded in the field of positive psychology and rationalized in the necessary understanding of a person's character traits, psychology teachers can provide students with meaningful learning experiences by having them engage in before-reading, during-reading, and after-reading activities with the anchor text, *Whale Talk*, which will allow students a deeper understanding of personality traits in action and how they contribute to the cohesion of a group community (i.e., on a sports team).

BEFORE READING *WHALE TALK*

In teaching a high school psychology class about the field of positive psychology, expounded upon above, psychology teachers could provide personal context for students' understandings of this strengths-based approach to personal growth and development before introducing YA literature. Before applying these VIA strengths to the characters in the YA novel, *Whale Talk*, students can take the VIA Survey for Youth on their own and learn the rankings of their own character strengths. In accordance with the psychology Personality Content Standard 1, which aims to provide students with perspectives on personality, students can be guided to evaluate trait theories (Content Standard 1.2), such as the character strengths system devised by Peterson and Seligman (2004). Teachers can guide students through analytical writing about these strengths by prompting them to write about their top five highest-ranked strengths and identify examples of how they use these strengths throughout their lives. Questions such as, "What life experiences have you had that demonstrate these strengths? What life stories can you share to teach these strengths to others? Why do you value this strength as contributing to your overall personality?" could serve as helpful prompts within a positive psychology framework for analysis. Students can also explore how they feel they have developed these strengths (e.g., from parents/guardians, school, sports, other life experiences) and consider how these strengths might be revealed in sports, games, and other competitions. In this before-reading activity, students meet both (a) literacy standards by writing arguments to support their claims about their own character traits through analysis of the application of these traits in their lives using valid reasoning and relevant and sufficient evidence and (b) psychology content standards (i.e., Personality Content Standard 2.1: Assessment of Personality) by assessing their personality traits through differentiated personality assessment techniques.

To make further connections to sports and other themes in *Whale Talk*, students could be asked to consider a situation when they participated in playing or watching sports and learned a positive life lesson. Through explanatory writing, students examine these complex ideas [and] concepts through the effective selection, organization, and analysis of content about the VIA Classification System of Virtues and Strengths to find relevance in their own lives. Additional prompts could include, "What was the lesson you learned? How could you apply this to other situations in your life? How did this lesson inform your understandings about teamwork and the group dynamics present within each group/ sports team? How does each person's strengths contribute to the overall productivity of the team?" In this way, students in a psychology class practice literacy in writing and are also given the opportunity to master *personality* Content Standard 3, Issues in Personality, by showing they are able to "analyze how individualistic and collectivistic cultural perspectives relate to personality" traits that they possess (Personality Content Standard 3.5). Examining the positive, unique contributions that each person can bring to a team's organization and success can also serve to show how personality traits not only serve people for their own personal growth but also for the benefit and collective good of a group, team, or society.

As a follow-up to this analytical writing activity, each student in the class could simultaneously engage in an inquiry project for which they are tasked with the responsibility of researching all the facets of one of the twenty-four character strengths—preferably one that is ranked as a "top 5 strength" in their survey results—and then teach that strength to the class. This research activity meets literacy standards for reading informational texts as students are asked to research and cite strong and thorough textual evidence to support their analysis of what the text says explicitly, about the traits they research, and make inferences about these traits in their presentations to the class. In their presentations, students could discuss (a) the definition of the strength (e.g., *zest*) as positive psychology has defined it (i.e., vitality, enthusiasm, vigor, energy, feeling alive, and activated), (b) the habits often exhibited by someone with that strength (i.e., a person with zest tends to possess a strong overall life satisfaction and tends to lead a life of engagement), and (c) the ways in which this strength can be developed by people who do not have this strength ranked as a high priority (i.e., as suggested on the VIA Institute on Character's [2016] website, in order to increase the amount of zest one possesses in life, a person could use the following strategies: "Improve your sleep hygiene by establishing regular sleep time, eating 3–4 hours before sleeping, avoiding doing any work in the bed, not taking caffeine late in the evening, etc."; "Notice changes in your energy level"; "Do a physically rigorous activity [bike riding, running, sports, singing, playing] that you always wanted to do but have not done yet"; and "Call [an] old friend and reminisce [about the] good old times.").

During this activity, students also demonstrate achievement of psychology *personality* Content Standard 3 as they research and present issues in personality and the degree of "stability and change" (3.2) possible for each character strength. Some traits may also provide opportunities for discussing "biological and situational influences" (Personality Content Standard 3.1) as well as "connections to health and work" (Personality Content Standard 3.3) and "self-concept" (Personality Content Standard 3.4). Teachers should also inform students that their "bottom 5" strengths ranked by the survey are not considered weaknesses, but rather are still strengths that are just not being as highly prioritized in their current circumstances (Peterson & Seligman, 2004). These strengths could rise in prominence as a person's life context shifts. It is important to make this distinction as positive psychology does not work within a deficit model, but rather is always a strengths-based approach to growth and development (Snyder et al., 2011).

During their reading of a YA novel, students can take their knowledge of these strengths and identify the ones they see are present in the characters of the novel. Often in works of YA sports literature, like in the novel *Whale Talk*, descriptions of a variety of team members are provided and distinct strengths in the characters emerge, which ultimately contribute to the success or cohesion of a team/group dynamic (i.e., Personality Content Standard 3.5: Analyze how individualistic and collectivistic cultural perspectives relate to personality). Seeing how each strength could benefit an individual and a team as a whole could be a worthwhile endeavor for students to explore together. Before being tasked with applying the VIA strengths to a character, however, students could also be given a pre-reading activity that allows them to explore the strengths of various professional athletes through a writing activity that encourages learning through vicarious experiences. First, students could brainstorm as a class a list of famous athletes or other athletes they know (e.g., in their families, at their schools) that possess positive characteristics and identify what some of those strengths might be. Then students could analyze as a class what makes each of these athletes positive role models. This applied writing and analysis activity also offers students opportunities to practice literacy by examining and conveying complex ideas, concepts, and information clearly and accurately through the effective selection, orga- nization, and analysis of content as well as Personality Content Standard 3.5 noted above.

To make this pre-reading activity more advanced, role-play components could be incorporated. According to Poorman (2002), role-playing activities increase student interest and understanding of content and can be used to enhance learning experiences for students in a variety of ways. For example, students could play the role of reporters and tell the inspiring stories of ath- letes they would like to highlight in a positive way in a news broadcast, or students could take on the role of the acclaimed athlete and share an award acceptance speech or hold a press conference where student reporters ask the athlete specific questions (Van Duinen, 2016). Students should be encouraged to write down talking points and questions related to their presentation and share with a partner in order to workshop broadcast/speech/press conference ideas. Teachers could then reserve the school auditorium for student presentations and designate a day in class for students to perform these role-playing scenarios to an audience of their peers. In multiple phases of this project, students are given various opportunities to master literacy standards that develop specific writing and speaking skills. To conclude this project, students could write a newspaper article (Fabrizi, 2016) about a famous athlete whose story made an impact on the audience, capitalizing on strengths that others might choose to emulate and what can be learned from this athlete that can inspire and motivate others in various ways (i.e., Personality Content Standard 3.5).

WHILE READING *WHALE TALK*

In Crutcher's (2001) *Whale Talk*, one of T.J.'s most vivid memories was the time when Mr. Simet, his English teacher and swim coach, mentioned that "any story is only true in the moment" (p. 10). The same can be said for the approach students can use to identify a character's virtues and strengths because as human beings, we are all constantly evolving and what we consider a strength at one moment may not feel much like a strength in another. In addition, as circumstances in life change, so do the strengths that we prioritize in our personality. Thus, the results of a person's VIA Strengths Survey may change from year to year or month to month depending on a person's particular situation and context (Peterson & Seligman, 2004). Though it may be difficult to explain this fluid nature of strengths to students over the course of a semester-long or even year-long psychology course by way of their own VIA Strengths survey results, it may be possible to demonstrate this phenomenon to students by using a YA novel that contains dynamic characters who change significantly throughout the timeline of the story. This will also enable students to "Differentiate personality assessment techniques" (Personality Content Standard 2.1) and "Discuss the reliability and validity of personality assessment techniques" (Personality Content Standard 2.2) over time. To help students examine this phenomenon through the dynamic strengths of characters in *Whale Talk*, consider the following approach.

First, read chapter one with students and ask them to pay specific attention to how the author characterizes T. J. Jones. This reading with a purpose activity allows students to analyze a complex set of ideas or sequence of events and explain how specific individuals, ideas, or events interact and develop over the course of the text while also applying psychology Personality Content Standard 2.1 (i.e., Differentiate personality assessment techniques). As students think back to the strengths from the VIA Survey for Youth, they may connect T.J. with strengths such as bravery, humor, integrity, leadership, and/ or perspective. As students read chapter one, consider providing them with a graphic organizer that invites them to complete four columns: (a) potential strength, (b) evidence of this strength, (c) quote that best exemplifies this strength, and (d) page number where evidence is located (adapted from Gibbons, n.d.). This use of a graphic organizer while reading also allows students to mindfully read with a purpose (Tovani, 2004), an important practice for close reading and analysis of textual support. After students have completed the graphic organizer, work together as a class to take the VIA Survey for Youth by role-playing the perspective of T.J. Jones. Students will then determine how the strengths they identified on their graphic organizer compare to T.J.'s survey results. Invite students to consider how each strength will benefit T.J. as an individual as well as the swim team he now represents. Be sure to save the results of this survey as they will be used later in the lesson.

After reading chapter one, assign each student a swim team member other than T.J. (i.e., Chris, Dan, Ta-Roy, Andy, Jackie, or Simon). Provide a fresh copy of the graphic organizer so students can begin to think about and find evidence of the strengths of their assigned character as they read the remainder of the text. The graphic organizer pertaining to T.J. will serve as a useful model for students as they consider their newly assigned character. Alert students that they will continue to return to T.J. as a whole class, but their attention throughout *Whale Talk* should be on considering the strengths of their individual character.

As readers, we learn a lot about T.J. Jones through the first six chapters of the text. After reading chapter six, discuss with students what they have learned about T.J.'s strengths and, as a group, retake the VIA Survey for Youth by once again role-playing T.J.'s perspective. Based on the results of the new survey, provide students with a two-circle Venn diagram so they can describe the commonalities and differences they notice in their survey findings. Ask students to reflect on Mr. Simet's statement when he said, "Any story is only true in the moment" (Crutcher, 2001, p. 10), and require them to use evidence from the survey results to consider how their findings were different in the moments after chapters 1 and 6. This will also serve to show the shifting nature of character strengths based on life circumstances, thus allowing students an opportunity to see how their own strengths may shift based on changes that may occur in their lives as well (Peterson & Seligman, 2004).

The team's first swim meet takes place in chapter eight of *Whale Talk* and provides a great deal of characterization about how each team member is characterized by the author and how each one interacts with his teammates. It is the perfect opportunity for students to work in common character groups to share what they have written on their graphic organizers. Then, ask students to individually role-play (Poorman, 2002) their respective character by taking the VIA Survey for Youth. Allow them to share their findings with their character groups to create a baseline for the character's strengths, and remind students that they must continue using the graphic organizer to consider their character's potential strengths throughout the remainder of the book. This use of the graphic organizer while reading also allows students to keep track of their literary analysis during group discussions as they cite evidence to support their analysis of what the text says explicitly, as well as inferences drawn from the text, including determining where the text leaves matters uncertain. Once the class has finished reading the book, work together as a class to complete a final VIA Survey for Youth for T.J.'s character, and remind them to consider Mr. Simet's statement, "Any story is only true in the moment" (Crutcher, 2001, p. 10), as students compare the results of T.J.'s three surveys. Finally, ask students to complete a final VIA Survey for Youth for their individual character and use the results to complete the forthcoming character profile. This activity combines two effective literacy strategies—reading with a purpose (Tovani, 2004) and role-playing (Poorman, 2002)—and provides an opportunity for close textual analysis through experiential learning practices.

AFTER READING *WHALE TALK*

After reading *Whale Talk*, invite students to create a character profile similar to the one described in Wickline's (n.d.) ReadWriteThink lesson plan entitled "Book Report Alternative: Getting Acquainted with Farcebook." White and Hungerford-Kresser (2014) describe the impact of social networking in the classroom as "a convenient tool that provides a culturally relevant and media rich space where meaning(s) can be negotiated and created" (p. 652). For the purposes of this activity, it may be helpful to use the web tool Farcebook (see Wickline, n.d.) or adapt the Farcebook profile to create a similar template that allows students to take greater advantage of the strengths they have identified for their specific characters (see also McClain, Brown, & Price, 2015, to consider the social networking tool Edmodo). Once students have created their character profile and compared notes with members of their character groups, utilize the jigsaw technique, an effective form of cooperative learning (Tran, 2014), by switching students into swim team groups so that each new group has every character from the swim team represented. Ask group members to share their individual character profiles with their new groups and to create a team profile that describes how the combined strengths of each character patterns together to form a successful team. In this post-reading activity, students are encouraged to consider why Crutcher may have created the team dynamics that he did in writing this YA novel by analyzing the impact of his choices. Through this analysis of team dynamics in the novel, students will also learn how important it is to form teams that include diverse people with a variety of strengths and personality traits in order to optimize success.

EXTENSION ACTIVITY BEYOND *WHALE TALK*

Digital video is one of the fastest-growing multimodal literacies located in secondary English classrooms (Miller & Bruce, 2017). Thus, an exciting possibility that meets countless ISTE Standards for Students (2016) is for students to work together in their new swim team groups to create a digital video starting lineup in which each character is highlighted as part of the team. Groups can use phones, tablets, or computers to record a video that includes each character saying his or her/per character name, swimming event, and one or two individual strengths that support the team as a collective unit. Encourage students to add some team uniforms, prerecorded pictures, exhilarating music, multimodal graphics, and/or background narration as needed, and teams can enter the room in style as they are introduced to the class via their video starting lineup. Teachers and students would need previous experience using Microsoft Moviemaker or iMovie or some other video production tool, although teachers who prefer a low-tech option could have students write the script for the video starting lineup and enact the performance in front of their peers.

CONCLUSION

Through the use of YA literature, psychology teachers can demonstrate to students the unique attributes of personality that contribute to the success of an individual and to the cohesion of a group. Using the VIA Strengths Survey for Youth, students can examine their own character strengths and evaluate to what extent they see these strengths as valid contributions to the teams they are members of. In addition, the shifting nature of a person's strengths based on life circumstances is an important concept for students to understand so they do not feel limited by or restricted to the particular expression of strengths they currently possess. By analyzing the changing strengths of characters in YA novels like *Whale Talk* and those listed above, students can learn through vicarious experiences the potential for adapting and developing new strengths as contexts in life shift as well.

Annotated List of Related YA Literature

The Perks of Being a Wallflower by Stephen Chobosky (224 pp.)

Fifteen-year-old Charlie is an introspective teenager, who makes friends with a group of older students who must collectively overcome issues ranging from drug use to mental health to sexual identity. Through this novel, students can analyze how certain character traits can serve as a buffer against certain behaviors that may be considered socially deviant or destructive.

The Outsiders by S. E. Hinton (192 pp.)

Two competing groups of young men, the greasers and the socs, are separated by social class. The greasers are generally defined as poor, social outcasts, while the socs are typically wealthier. The story revolves around the experiences of fourteen-year-old Ponyboy Curtis, a greaser forced to grow up much too quickly. In reading this novel, students can explore how social class may influence the development of character strengths and how the dynamics of a group can lead to the prominence of some strengths over others.

Openly Straight by Bill Konisgberg (336 pp.)

Rafe, a high school soccer player, transfers to an all-boys' boarding school in New England in order to keep his sexuality a secret and separate from his athletic identity. The book explores Rafe's desire to be identified by other strengths he possess, like his athleticism, at his new school, despite the fact that he had always previously identified as openly gay. Through an analysis of Rafe's multiple character strengths and how they manifest in his schooling experiences, students can explore why Rafe chooses to keep his sexuality a secret at his new school and how his character strengths change throughout the novel.

To Kill a Mockingbird by Harper Lee (384 pp.)

Scout and Jem, the children of Atticus Finch, seek to understand various issues of right and wrong in the small town of Maycomb, Alabama, during the Great Depression. Because this novel is so frequently taught in English classrooms across the United States, analyzing the work through a positive psychology lens may provide a newer approach to teaching this work. Students can engage in various methods of character strength analysis by using the VIA Survey for Youth when evaluating the children in the novel and by using the VIA Survey for Adults in evaluating Atticus and the other adults. Then, students can examine how the personality traits of each character interact throughout the novel to teach the children, the adults, and the entire town important lessons of civility, humility, and humanity.

Roll of Thunder, Hear My Cry by Mildred D. Taylor (288 pp.)

Nine-year-old Cassie Logan and her family live in rural Mississippi during the Depression and face racial discrimination at every turn as they struggle to maintain control of their land. The dynamics of the characters in this novel can be explored by having students complete the VIA Survey for each character and evaluate how these strengths helped the characters to forge forward in the struggles they experience.

REFERENCES

American Psychological Association (2011). National Standards for High School Psychology Curricula. Washington, DC: APA. Retrieved from http://www.apa.org/education/k12/psychology-curricula.pdf.

Chobosky, S. (1999). *The perks of being a wallflower*. New York: Pocket Books.

Crutcher, C. (2001). *Whale talk*. New York: Greenwillow Books.

Fabrizi, M. (2016). A flair for sports: Teaching journalistic writing using a 3–2–1 column approach. In A. Brown & L. Rodeliser (Eds.), *Developing contemporary literacies through sports: A guide for the English classroom*, 86–92. Urbana, IL: National Council of Teachers of English.

Gibbons, L. A. (n.d.). Creating psychological profiles of characters in *To Kill a Mockingbird*. Retrieved from http://www.readwritethink.org/classroom-resources/lesson-plans/creating-psychological-profiles-characters-1184.html.

Hinton, S. E. (1967). *The outsiders*. New York: Viking Press.

International Society for Technology in Education (2016). ISTE Standards for Students. Arlington, VA: ISTE. Retrieved from https://www.iste.org/standards/standards/for-students-2016.

Konisgberg, B. (2015). *Openly straight*. New York: Arthur A. Levine Books.

Lee, H. (1982). *To kill a mockingbird*. New York: Warner Books.

Lipsyte, R. (2011, July 27). Jocks vs. pukes: Jock culture is a distortion of sports. *The Nation* (August 15–22, 2011 issue). Retrieved from https://www.thenation.com/article/jocks-vs-pukes/.

McClain, C., Brown, A., & Price, G. (2015). *Characterization personified: Using Edmodo to strengthen student interaction with literature. Meridian, 18*. Retrieved from https://www.ced.ncsu.edu/meridian/index.php/meridian/article/view/74.

Miller, S., & Bruce, D. (2017). Welcome to the 21st century: New literacies stances to support student learning with digital video composing. *English Journal, 106*(3), 14–18.

Peterson, C., & Seligman, M. E. P. (2004). *Character strengths and virtues: A handbook and classification*. Washington, DC: American Psychological Association.

Poorman, P. B. (2002). Biography and role-playing: Fostering empathy in abnormal psychology. *Teaching of Psychology, 29*(1), 32–36.

Snyder, C. R., Lopez, S. J., & Pedrotti, J. T. (2011). *Positive psychology: The scientific and practical explorations of human strengths* (2nd ed.). Thousand Oaks, CA: Sage Publications.

Taylor, M. D. (2001). *Roll of thunder, hear my cry*. New York: Random House.

Tovani, C. (2004). *Do I really have to teach reading?* Portland, ME: Stenhouse Publishers.

Tran, V. D. (2014). The effects of cooperative learning on the academic achievement and knowledge retention. *International Journal of Higher Education, 3*(2), 131–140.

Van Duinen, D. V. (2016). Being the expert: Recognizing and developing students' insider sports knowledge. In A. Brown & L. Rodeliser (Eds.), *Developing contemporary literacies through sports: A guide for the English classroom*, 199–204. Urbana, IL: National Council of Teachers of English.

VIA Institute on Character (2017). *The VIA survey.* Retrieved from http://www. viacharacter.org/www/The-Survey.

White, J. W., & Hungerford-Kresser, H. (2014). Character journaling through social networks. *Journal of Adolescent & Adult Literacy, 57*(8), 642–654.

Wickline, K. (n.d.). *Book report alternative: Getting acquainted with Facebook.* Retrieved from http://www.readwritethink.org/classroom-resources/lesson-plans/book-report-alternative-getting-30874.html.

About the Editors

Paula Greathouse, PhD, is an assistant professor of secondary English education at Tennessee Tech University. She was a secondary English and reading teacher for sixteen years. She is an active member of National Council of Teachers of English (NCTE), American Educational Research Association (AERA), and a state representative for Assembly on Literature for Adolescents (ALAN). She sits on NCTE's Standing Committee against Censorship, LGBT Advisory Committee, and Gender and Equities Committee. She has won several awards including the Florida Council of Teachers of English High School Teacher of the Year Award and NCTE Teacher of Excellence Award.

Joan F. Kaywell, PhD, is professor of English education at the University of South Florida (USF) where she has won several teaching awards for her passion of assisting preservice and practicing teachers in discovering ways to improve literacy. She donates her time extensively to the National Council of Teachers of English (NCTE), its affiliate FCTE, and is past president of NCTE's Assembly on Literature for Adolescents (ALAN). She is highly published with fourteen textbooks to her credit, most recently (with Michael Anthony) *Between the Lines: Actively Engaging Readers in the English Classroom* (Rowman & Littlefield, 2016). She was the recipient of the 2012 ALAN Hipple Award for Outstanding Service and the 2010 NCTE Conference on English Leadership (CEL) Exemplary Leadership Award, and FCTE established the Joan F. Kaywell "Literature Saves Lives" Book Award to honor her for her "deep commitment to FCTE, the profession, and her fervent belief in young adult (YA) literature."

Brooke Eisenbach, PhD, is assistant professor of middle and secondary education at Lesley University. She was a middle school English and YA literature teacher for nine years and an English I virtual school teacher for two years. She is an active member of National Council of Teachers of English (NCTE) and American Educational Research Association (AERA), and serves as a state representative for ALAN. She is a member of NCTE's Standing Committee against Censorship. She has won several awards including the Florida Council of Teachers of English Teacher of the Year Award and the NCTE Outstanding Middle Level Educator in the English Language Arts Award.

About the Contributors

James E. Akenson, PhD, teaches elementary and secondary social studies methods courses at Tennessee Technological University in Cookeville. He also teaches graduate social studies courses as well as a graduate level course for teachers on integrating country music in the K-12 curriculum. Akenson is an active member of the Tennessee Council for the Social Studies (TCSS), serving on its board of directors and served as president and executive director.

Isaac Bickmore is a doctoral student in music education at Arizona State University (ASU). He taught general music and choir for five years in Salt Lake City at a kindergarten through eighth-grade school. He has taught and is currently teaching in the Digital Hybrid Lab at ASU, which is a class that examines the intersection of music, teaching, and technology.

Steven T. Bickmore, PhD, is an associate professor of English education at the University of Nevada Las Vegas (UNLV) and maintains a weekly academic blog on YA literature. He is a past editor of *The ALAN Review* and a founding editor of *Study and Scrutiny: Research in Young Adult Literature.*

Paul E. Binford, PhD, is an assistant professor in the Department of Curriculum, Instruction & Special Education at Mississippi State University (MSU). He served as both a middle school and high school teacher and administrator from 1985 to 2011 while earning his PhD from Indiana University. Dr. Binford's scholarly work on the history of the social studies and cross-curricular connections has appeared in a variety of journals, including *Theory and Research in Social Education, International Journal of Social Education, American Educational History Journal, Sound Historian, Louisiana English Journal*, and *The ALAN Review.*

Alan Brown, PhD, is an assistant professor of English education and the secondary education program coordinator in the Department of Education at Wake Forest University. Dr. Brown is also a former high school English teacher and basketball coach.

Kristy A. Brugar, PhD, is an assistant professor at the University of Oklahoma where she teaches social studies education courses. Prior to working at the university level, she was a middle school social studies teacher in Maryland and Michigan.

Chris Crowe, PhD, teaches adolescent literature and creative writing at Brigham Young University (BYU). He is a former high school English teacher and the author of many articles and several books, including the historical novel that is the subject of chapter that discusses *Mississippi Trial, 1955*.

Mike DiCicco, PhD, is an assistant professor of literacy education at Northern Kentucky University and former middle school language arts and reading teacher.

Brooke Eisenbach, PhD, is an assistant professor of middle and secondary education at Lesley University. She was a middle school English and YA literature teacher for nine years and an English I virtual school teacher for two years. She is an active member of National Council of Teachers of English (NCTE) and American Educational Research Association (AERA) and serves as a state representative for ALAN. She is a member of NCTE's Standing Committee against Censorship. She has won several awards including the Florida Council of Teachers of English Teacher of the Year Award and the NCTE Outstanding Middle Level Educator in the English Language Arts Award.

Melissa Gross, PhD, is professor and doctoral program chair in the School of Information Studies at Florida State University and past president of the Association for Library and Information Science Education (ALISE). Dr. Gross has published extensively in the areas of information seeking behavior, information literacy, library program and service evaluation, information resources for youth, and teacher/librarian collaboration.

A. Suzie Henning, PhD, is an assistant professor of foundations at Eastern Washington University where she currently serves as the director of undergraduate programs and field experiences in the education department. Her teaching focuses on social studies methods, assessment and foundations, and educational equity.

Crag Hill, PhD, is the English education coordinator at the University of Oklahoma. His scholarly work includes two edited collections from Routledge: *Teaching Comics through Multiple Lenses: Critical Perspectives* (2016) and *The Critical Merits of Young Adult Literature: Coming of Age* (2014). He also is the coeditor of an online, open access journal devoted to empirical and critical scholarship on young adult literature, *Study and Scrutiny: Research on Young Adult Literature*.

Elizabeth Brendel Horn, MFA, is an assistant professor in the graduate Theatre for Young Audiences Program at the University of Central Florida (UCF). She works as a freelance director, teaching artist, consultant, dramaturge, and applied theater artist, having worked with the Orlando Repertory Theatre, Orlando Shakespeare Theatre, The Coterie, Dr. Phillips Center for the Arts, and Orange County Public Schools. Elizabeth is published with *Youth Theatre Journal*, *TYA Today*, and *Theatre Topics* and serves on the boards of TYA/USA and Florida Theatre Conference.

Katie Irion is a former high school English teacher who is currently pursuing her graduate degree in English from Brigham Young University.

Robert Jordan is a former middle-grade English language arts teacher and current doctoral candidate in English Education at the University of South Florida.

Jeffrey S. Kaplan, PhD, is an associate professor emeritus for the School of Teaching, Learning, and Leadership in the College of Education and Human Performance at the University of Central Florida. Recently, he coedited with Judith Hayn, *Teaching Young Adult Literature Today: Insights, Considerations and Perspectives for the Classroom Teacher* (Rowman & Litttlefield, 2012, 2016), *Young Adult Nonfiction: Gateway to the Common* Core (Rowman & Littlefield, 2015), and *Teaching Young Adult Literature: Integrating, Implementing and Re-Imagining the Common Core* (Rowman & Littlefield, 2015). Active in the study of self-study and reflective practice, he and Elsie Olan, PhD, codirect the Laboratory for the Study of Holistic Teaching and Learning at the University of Central Florida.

Don Latham, PhD, is a professor in the School of Information at Florida State University (FSU). Dr. Latham has published extensively on information behavior of young adults, digital literacies, and YA literature and literacy practices. He teaches courses in Information Needs of Children, Information Needs of Young Adults, and Graphic Novels in Libraries.

Malinda Hoskins Lloyd, PhD, is in her twenty-seventh year in the field of education. She currently teaches or has taught literacy, mathematics, science, and social studies methods courses at Tennessee Tech University.

Jason L. O'Brien, PhD, is an associate professor in the College of Education at the University of Alabama in Huntsville. His research interests include teaching ELs more effectively, citizenship education, and experiential pedagogy in the classroom.

Luke Rumohr is a junior high world geography and U.S. history teacher in Cadillac, Michigan. He has fourteen years of classroom experience in late elementary and middle-level education and is currently teaching eighth-graders.

Gretchen Rumohr-Voskuil, PhD, is an associate professor of English and the writing program administrator at Aquinas College, where she teaches writing and language arts methods courses.

Shelly Shaffer, PhD, is an assistant professor of literacy in the Department of Education at Eastern Washington University where she teaches preservice elementary and secondary teachers. She has taught Content Area Literacy and Writing, secondary methods, several YA Literature and Children's Literature courses, and graduate research courses.

Nicole Sieben, EdD, is an assistant professor of secondary English education and the coordinator for the graduate programs in English education at SUNY College at Old Westbury. She is a former high school English teacher in New York public schools and is the current chair of the National Council for Teachers of English (NCTE) Genders and Sexualities Equality Alliance (GSEA).

Julie Stepp, PhD, is professor for the graduate concentration in School Library Science in the College of Education at Tennessee Tech University.

Shelbie Witte, PhD, is an associate professor of adolescent literacy and the Chuck and Kim Watson Endowed Chair in education at Oklahoma State University. Dr. Witte has published extensively on the literacy lives of adolescents, particularly middle school students at the intersection of literacy and popular culture. She directs the OSU Writing Project and is coeditor (with Sara Kajder) of NCTE's *Voices from the Middle*.

Author and Title Index

Subject Index